What people are saying about...

From Sin and Sorrow to Service

Kay Painter joins the remarkable cadre of twenty-first century voices proclaiming the victorious transformation from the kingdom of darkness to God's Kingdom of love! The pain of abortion is being replaced with the hope and promise of a life in Christ, and Kay's testimony is a how to guide. A must read.

Dr. Alveda C. King
King for America and Priests for Life.

Many have shared in at least some of Kay's hardships. But be encouraged. Her passion for Christ is the fruit of God's amazing grace in her redeemed life. I am confident this book will minister to your heart, regardless of where you've been and where you are now.

Brad Mattes
Brad is the Executive Director of Life Issues Institute and a two-time Emmy® Award winning TV host of Facing Life Head-On. He is also the radio voice for Life Issues, a daily commentary on over 1,100 outlets.

This book is a stunning reminder of God's endless mercy. Kay's story is told with such courage and honesty that it was impossible for me to put it down. Even though I have never personally gone through some of the stuff she talks about in this book, her openness and vulnerability made me feel like I could relate to her. Many people sitting in churches are holding onto deep, dark secrets that they are afraid to confess because they are afraid of being judged by others. Sadly, I have heard Christian women say, "God could never forgive me for this." This book is a must read for any woman who is struggling with moving on from or letting go of sins of her past. It is a must read for Christians who feel forgiveness is out of their reach and it is a must read for anyone who has forgotten that God's mercy, love and peace know no limits.

Jaime Thietten
Contemporary Christian Recording Artist

It takes a special kind of brave to bare your life to the reading public and Kay Painter has it. Her heartfelt plea of "here I am Lord, look at me, change me, make me Yours" is ringing out page by page as she exposes the darkest, rawest parts of her life before seeing the Light - the one true Light. Kay leads us down the path of her life - falling into the trap of abortion, tripping into adultery, stumbling into divorce, before finally taking firm hold of the hand of God as He rescued her and set her down upon the solid ground of His Way.

This book will act like a large illuminated "Danger Ahead" sign to warn others to be far more careful where they tread in order to stay on the right path rather than suffer as Kay has done, crawling through the brambles of life to get back to it! The clear message of the book is that no matter how far down the wrong road you go, you can always turn around.

Teresa Martin
State President, Cherish Life Queensland Inc.,
Brisbane, Australia

From Sin

And Sorrow

To Service

The Journey of God's Prodigal Daughter

Kay Painter

From Sin and Sorrow to Service

By Kay Painter

First Edition: February 2013
ISBN (Print):   978-1-938596-11-7
ISBN (Kindle):   978-1-938596-12-4
ISBN (ePub):   978-1-938596-13-1

Original cover design by Carrie Lynn.
Cover illustration by Hannah Slick.
Cover enhancements by Ray Ellis II.

Published in the United States of America
NCC Publishing
Meridian, Idaho, 83642, USA
www.nccpublishing.com

8397114972013020204

I dedicate this book in memory of my husband, Doug, who celebrated his first Christmas in the presence of his Lord in December 2012.

K

A full dedication to Doug, and his life of service, is included at the end of this book.

Foreword

I first met Kay when she came to the Pregnancy Center training meetings to become a volunteer counselor. She was like a racehorse—eager to be turned loose at the starting gate, a sponge wanting to soak in everything possible so she could love the women and girls who would find themselves at the center of an unplanned pregnancy situation. Her reason for wanting to help was because she had experienced an unplanned pregnancy and had a strong desire to help others make a better choice than she did.

I recall many conversations with Kay in which she expressed how much she enjoyed helping the women at Lifeline, but she always felt like there was more she should be doing. She just didn't know what. Her faith in God's leading and using her story to help others soon opened doors she had no way of opening on her own; it was only by God's hand in her life and His answering her prayers to "use me and my story, Lord."

What came next was a whirlwind of opportunities: speaking to women's groups, traveling to other countries, speaking out at Pro-Life rallies, and meeting some important and influential people. One might think that was enough. Her ministry was impacting more people than Kay ever dreamed—but no! What you are holding in your hands right now was the next step God had planned for Kay.

Again, God took the lead and Kay obeyed. A book could reach more people than Kay ever could personally. In this book she lets you get to know about her beginnings, and what transpired in her life to put her where she is now. You will witness a humbleness that only God can birth in someone as she has experienced life in ways that many of us will never know. As you open the pages and read Kay's story, open your heart as well. Let it give you hope that there is a light at the end of the tunnel, even if you have a similar story.

Knowing Kay, it doesn't matter if this book becomes a bestseller. What matters is that the right person reads the book—the one who needs forgiveness and to be set free. When that happens, Kay will know she has the Father's approval of her obedience in following His leading, and she has done what HE has asked of her. The question is, Are you the person this book is written for?

Lastly, pass the book on to bring restoration to someone else. A book on a shelf does no good. Enjoy your journey with Kay; remember the many *Saras* as she has—ones no one has written about.

Linda Stradley
Co-Director, Lifeline Pregnancy Center

Humble Acknowledgments

To the only true living God: the same God of Abraham, Isaac, and Jacob. The only God who voluntarily sent His only Son to die in my place, that I, in my sin, might be free. Jeshua, who pursued me, changed my life and with whom I will eventually live forever. God, through His people, without exception, has supplied for every trip *completely*, even when expenses run far over expectations. If He calls, He will provide. Who can imagine how differently this story would have concluded without Him. No words, no works, no thanks, no sacrifice can even begin to express what I owe Him.

Doug: my godly husband, who is my covering, my advisor, my best friend, and helpmate. He has celebrated with me, held me as I cried, encouraged me, and paid the cost of Remembering S.A.R.A. Ministries International—a ministry in its infancy stages. He is my technical advisor, computer expert, and "I'll-Fix-It-Man" who constantly provides a voice of reason when I would get myself in trouble. Doug unselfishly allows me freedom to leave our little home without complaint whenever and wherever I am called . . . always there to greet me with his big smile and warm arms upon my return (sometimes even with roses). He is one of the greatest gifts God has given me, outside of His Son and my children.

My three wonderful kids—Suzie, DeeDee, and Kevin: They have been instrumental in allowing me to share my story in its entirety and still love me— who were sometimes victims of my selfishness. They paid a dear price for being mine and, yet today, are enjoying their own personal journeys with our Lord. I love you each so very much. And to those not mine by blood, but by choice, who call me "Mom." What an unwarranted gift you bring as we graft our lives into an extended family. You, too, have added joy and wonder to this family.

Carrie Lynn: (Not her real name—she wants credit to go to her Heavenly Father.) A great friend, but who has become far more. Carrie is just one of the "daughters" whose life has been divinely woven into ours. She was instrumental in changing the depth of this book with her training and hours of dedication. Her heart's desire is to help others accept Christ as their personal Savior and receive the gift of freedom they so desperately need. No words are adequate to express her part in this book.

Hannah: young, beautiful, and talented, yet only sixteen years old. With insecurity and doubt and prayer, she created the illustration on this book cover. She freely gave of her talent and time, so this book could change lives. Be blessed, Hannah.

Linda: who volunteered to edit the compilation to complete the circle her husband began when he counseled me through all my guilt. Her prayers, smile, and encouragement were also invaluable in producing this book.

To three special ladies at the pregnancy center: Linda, who wrote the foreword; Diann, who allowed me to begin this walk with baby steps at the center; Willy, who let me sit with her for hours and siphon knowledge and wisdom from her seventeen years of counseling experience. Guiding and directing me, she taught me how to advance others through their pain. To these three ladies, whose encouragement and faith propelled me into more service with self-confidence, and who were also the first to offer me a public stage on which I could begin my ministry. I pledge 10 percent of all the profits of this book as more resources for them to meet the needs of young girls in unexpected pregnancies, or post-abortive ladies (like myself) who need to find Christ and forgiveness.

Pastor Randy: who saw a passion for sharing my testimony I did not see in myself. He responded to the call he saw in my life. Then he offered to me a ministry, which extended from the church for support and provided guidelines on which to build that ministry. Without his foresight, Remembering S.A.R.A. Ministries International may not have reached the millions of people it has today.

A second Pastor Randy: who, with no benefit for himself or his church, has been a constant tower of strength and encouragement to me in so many ways. I believe he will be rewarded by our Heavenly Father for his commitment to Remembering S.A.R.A. Ministries International. You have my gratitude.

The ladies of my accountability group: who pray unceasingly for this ministry, offer suggestions, and sometimes say, "No." I am forever indebted.

My advisory group: who pray constantly and hold me accountable for personal actions, ministerial actions, and attitudes.

Friends: who have stood by me, even after I revealed all the ugly, despicable details of the life I once led, who still call me friend. Many support Remembering S.A.R.A. Ministries International with financial help. I take the responsibility quite seriously in deciding the way I spend it for the kingdom. May the sacrifice of your gifts be rewarded by a Heavenly Father who created and owns even the glimmering stars, the earth, and all that dwell upon it.

My sincerest thanks and gratitude to all of you,

K

From
Sin

And
Sorrow

To
Service

Sin

Chapter One

Cindy, my friend from Louisiana and roommate in Washington, D.C., seemed as bewildered as I was as she said it: "Kay, God just gave me a message for you. It was very clear," she continued, "I am to tell you, 'Go, prepare, build stamina both physically and spiritually, for I have a journey for you.'"

My eyes welled with tears as we climbed into our beds, trying to rationalize what had just happened. I could not help but wonder if it was part of the puzzle God had been revealing to me with some incidents that had been occurring on this trip. Some unusual coincidences appeared to be leading me in an, as yet, unknown direction. But the hour was late, and in the warmth of the silky bed and cloud-like pillows, we both soon drifted off into a deep childlike sleep.

It had been a lengthy and exhausting, yet exhilarating day. As the March for Life moved up Pennsylvania Avenue, headed for the Supreme Court, crisp, cold air kissed our faces and our breath transformed into vapor as we walked. Intermittent snowflakes fell softly, landing gently on our faces, only to melt and vanish. They seemed to affirm God's promise: "Though your sins are like scarlet, they shall be as white as snow" (Isaiah 1:18). This was all so new for me—to see the obvious; only in retrospect would I clearly see His fingerprints all over this event in my life.

Although I had not yet admitted to the world that I had an abortion, I had long dreamed of participating in the March for Life, and the experience was more than I could have ever imagined. Brilliant beams of light streaming through the dark clouds made the day all the more memorable. Then the finale—the promise from God. After all I had done against Him, He was aware of me. Even though I did not understand its meaning or comprehend what lay ahead, the Creator loved me so much He had spoken just to me.

Morning found me boarding my flight, returning to home and to reality. My mind replayed over and over the phenomenon of the night before, wondering where it might lead. Once in the air, I laid my head back and closed my eyes. Time seemed to stop. It was apparent God was in charge of this moment. Taking a deep breath, I wondered what He had in mind. It was then God began to give me a peek at what lay ahead. Little did I know what all He was about to disclose to me.

I was indeed headed for a journey. As with any trip, I needed to prepare by gathering and packing what would be needed and disposing of that which would be of no use. Guilt. Shame. Self-destruction. All would have to be thrown out and discarded. But the lessons I had learned from all the pain of sin, and the answers I had found in response to my experiences, I would pack and repack these epiphanies, using them over and over again for God's glory by sharing them with others.

With thoughts of the promise God had given to me still fresh in my mind and heart, new excitement rose within me. To move forward into His plan, God began to uncover the hidden parts of my life I had buried deep within. I needed to resolve the many shadows still binding me to the past. I would need to meet and deal directly with some of the dark memories. Though it was unspoken, I had complete assurance He would help me through it all. The show was about to start.

It ran like an autobiography turned movie. Reliving my sordid past, I appeared as an actress in a film, depicting memories of "the me" who no longer existed. The bleak pages and chaotic chapters of my life unfolded on my mind's screen. The scenes were from a life of self-centeredness, sin, and sorrow. All the repulsiveness, the disgraceful actions, the prideful decisions, and the pain came to the forefront of my consciousness as God played them before me. He led me tenderly, one scene at a time. It became vividly apparent I had chosen the long, desolate path. At the same time, I was sharply *aware that my God was preparing to give me a brand-new start.*

The movie opened with scenes from the last of my teenage years, as I headed off into adulthood, leaving God far behind....

After school and on Saturdays, during my last two years of high school, I was the girl working behind the soda fountain counter in our local drug store, much like a scene from TV's *Happy Days*. One Saturday, in walked a tall, handsome young man I had met the previous week at the town bowling alley. Jeffrey asked me out, and I soon told my best friend, "I think I will marry him." Only a few, short months later, I did just that.

Encouraged by my parents, I had considered college, thinking I might become an English teacher. But money was short, and nouns and verbs, singular and plural, were no longer my priority. My heart had been stolen; I wanted to marry and begin a family of my own. We planned our wedding for September. Although I had enjoyed dating many young men over the past few years, even having been proposed to two times, I promised myself I would remain pure for my wedding night. I began married life as a very naïve twenty-year-old.

Not once did I ask my Heavenly Father about His plan for my life. All the wisdom I had heard and learned as a child in a Christian home receded to the farthest corners of my mind. Jeff was not a Christian, but had agreed to attend church with me. The teachings I had heard like, "equally yoked" seemed immaterial. Jeff was a great guy; I could make a few adjustments in him once we were married. I was sure we would live a fairy-tale life, happily ever after. How different my future might have been had I sought answers in God's Word and in prayer, but for years I would do things my way. So I stepped into marriage with both eyes wide shut and my heart ruling my head. It was the beginning of a long pattern of behaviors with me.

My new mother-in-law, battling brain cancer, was unable to attend the wedding. We had promised to stop by the hospital before leaving on our honeymoon. Sleeping when we arrived, she looked extremely fragile, and her breathing was shallow. We waited, hoping she would awaken. After some time it seemed apparent she would not wake. So, leaving a note, we headed for our beach house honeymoon, anticipating a full week of memories to be made.

We called in daily to check the prognosis. On the third day, we received word Jeff's mother was fading away. Scurrying to get back, we went directly to the hospital, but she had slipped into a coma. Later that night, her pain and struggle ended peacefully.

Jeff had unspeakable remorse for not being able to say "Goodbye." It was the first time I had seen him cry uncontrollably. How helpless I felt. On our first week anniversary, the family gathered again in the same church, but this time it was not the festive event it had been the previous week. Little did I know then how often I would be compared to, and expected to live up to, the quiet lady remembered that day.

Jeff and I attended my hometown church regularly, spending Sunday afternoons with my parents. Jeff became the son my father was never able to raise. My parents had a baby boy many years before, who died shortly after birth. A pastor told them if they had not baptized the two-day-old, then their baby boy was in hell. My father's response was, "If that is the God I serve, I'll go to hell and be with my son!" Now, because of my husband's influence, my father was again attending church. Both of the important men in my life accepted Jesus as their Savior and on one incredible Sunday, were baptized on the same day.

Even with this outward symbol of inside changing (baptism), I must admit neither Jeff nor I noticeably changed our spiritual lives. We did not bother to ask God about His plan for our lives. We did not seek Him in any way. Often we left the Word riding in the backseat of our car. That is a good thing, right? Keeping the Bible handy for the next time we would need it? At least we would not be without it the next Sunday—it was easily accessible…on the backseat of the car.

Oh, sure, there were times when life became complicated, and we would pray, asking God to help us out. We considered ourselves *good people*. We gave reverence to God on His day, as we should. But we did not ask for, or even think we needed, God's directives on how to live. It would be a long time before I would discover He was my only answer.

❧⟨∞⟩❧

Three years after we married, we proudly announced we would be giving my parents their first grandchild. The atmosphere was indescribable, dripping with joy and expectancy. Then just weeks before our baby was due, my dad came home from work having chest pains. That night we visited with him at the hospital, and he patted my swollen tummy as I kissed him good night. As we walked past his window, he rose up to wave to us. Just about midnight the call came; my daddy had moved on to join the Lord. Sadly, he would never experience the thrill of holding his tiny, new granddaughter, Susan, who arrived just two weeks later. At the time I recall knowing my daddy was safely in the arms of the Lord; his true love of Jesus permeated every area of his life and was obvious to everyone who knew him.

Suzie was our pride and joy! Just to see her little smile would give us goose bumps. If she would cry, it almost crushed our hearts. Like most parents, we considered this perfect little girl we had created to be everything. She was all we had dreamed of and more. Jeff and I wanted to be the best parents in the world for this beautiful new life that had been given to us. Neither of us realized how wise or necessary it should have been to seek guidance from a loving Heavenly Father. Unfortunately, He was never invited into our home or considered to be part of our daily lives. And Jesus is such a gentleman: He never forces Himself on anyone, never stays where He is not welcome—no matter how much He desires to be present.

❧⟨∞⟩❧

Although *gone,* my mother-in-law was still very much a part of our lives. Jeff would constantly tell me about his mother's precedents: After working in the fields all day, she would fix a supper (which ALWAYS included meat and potatoes) for her family and then *unwind* by working in her rose garden until dark. This was her life, day after day after day.

Me? I hated hoeing alone—hundreds of rows ahead of me. Working acres of berries and being expected to keep them weed free was not easy. I was tired and cranky when mealtime finally arrived. As for maintaining a flower garden—forget it! Jeff repeatedly reminded me I was expected to continue his mother's legacy; I gritted my teeth and worked harder.

Spring arrived and the farm that Jeff and his family owned demanded even more attention. My mother moved in with us to help care for Suzie and free up my time to help work the farm. Her presence was a blessing throughout the spring, summer, and especially during harvest. Her assistance left me time to be a wife to Jeff, mother to Suzie, and farmhand when needed—aspirations individually not easily met, much less in tandem. Each evening my mother would have the house clean. She also prepared meals for us all, including my father-in-law, Carl, who regularly joined us.

The end of harvest was an occasion to celebrate! The four of us decided to enjoy an evening out, filled with fun and laughter. Driving home at its conclusion, I was shocked to peer into the backseat to discover my father-in-law and mother holding hands. I was disgusted, hurt, and angry! How could my mom betray my father like that! Upon arriving home, I informed Jeff to advise his father to keep his hands off my mom.

Mom and I had some extensive talks, and I subsequently began to recognize how selfish my attitude had been. She had kept her wedding vows until my father's death. But now my dad was gone, and she was lonely. In Carl she had found someone to fill the empty spot in her heart. After we talked, I realized the glimmer in her eyes and the content smile, which recently appeared on her face, had been missing since my father's death. Even as an adult, marriage of your parent is an arduous adjustment to make. But since I loved her, I wanted her to be happy.

⚜

The next August found me once again standing before our pastor. I was my mother's matron of honor, while Jeff stood as best man beside his father. How we would chuckle thinking of the song, "I'm My Own Grandpa." It was almost true: My husband was now my stepbrother; my mother was also my mother-in-law; my brother-in-law was also my stepbrother. We often wondered if Suzie was our niece as well as our daughter! It made for interesting coffee chat, if nothing else.

❧ *Chapter Two* ❧

Not long after Suzie was born, I began to notice changes in our marriage. I knew Jeff's brother had a terrible temper, but I never thought the same might be true of Jeff. During almost a year of dating, Jeff seemed shy, almost bashful; the angry side of him had remained hidden. Now Jeff's temper reared its ugly head more and more frequently.

In spite of the outbursts, Jeff and I desperately wanted to have another child, but I was unable to conceive. Doctors could find nothing wrong, and after numerous tests, they simply said, "You just may not get pregnant again." Both Jeff and I had been late-in-life babies from our parents, virtually a second family. We had been raised more like single children, but we wanted companionship for Suzie. We wanted her to have a sister with whom to grow up, to love, to play with, and even to share. We were realistic enough to know there would also be the typical sibling disagreements over toys, cookies, and clothing.

We began the adoption process, completing our paperwork and waiting expectantly for the next step—the personal interviews. They were *very* personal! We were interviewed together and individually, asked questions about our sex life, and on one visit, the social worker even opened our dresser drawers and searched our attic. We both wanted to challenge the encroachment of our privacy but did not want to jeopardize our chances for a baby. We bit our tongues and smiled. I was so fearful of Jeff's temper during this long period of stress. Perhaps because of the sincere desire we both had to have additional children, he kept it well in check.

I kept thinking another set of feet in the house would fill the ever-growing emptiness I felt. The day finally arrived when the case worker handed us our prospective new daughter. One look at her and we both fell in love: beautiful golden-blond hair with just a couple curls flowing down her back, the biggest and deepest blue eyes full of wonder. The county had been unable to locate the baby's biological father, so she was ineligible for adoption until after a one-year waiting period. Oddly enough, we began the process of intruding, awkward interviews and inspections just about the time she was born. Once we held her, there was no question she was meant to be ours. We wanted to take her home right then and there, but were forced to wait thirty days to be sure we would not change our minds. We were, however, granted three-hour visitations once a week to help her with the adjustments that were just ahead.

While we excitedly counted the days of that very long month, Jeff intermittently continued to find fault with my actions or suggestions. Although to me, they were very trivial things; the verbal abuse on these issues told me they were critical issues to him. A new physical component to his temper, although infrequent, was becoming more and more of a concern.

Deidra Ann came to us on the day after her first birthday. I will always remember the surge of emotions that swept through me as this innocent, helpless toddler was handed to me. From the minute I held her, I knew she would be the next addition to our family, and we would not relinquish this young child. However, this huge, dramatic change was one in which Deidra herself had no choice. Deidra was merely snatched from the arms of the foster parents she had known for the last few months and handed over to us with little more than "Here she is."

It was completely overwhelming to me to realize how one minute we were visitors, then seconds later, responsible for her. It was also disappointing as we observed how callously this *transaction* was handled with regard to Deidra's feelings, fears, and expectations. With her worldly possessions collected in a single paper shopping bag and totally without a voice in her own destiny, Deidra's only action was to search my eyes with a questioning, penetrating look in her own blue eyes. We scurried home to where grandparents, aunts, uncles, cousins, and friends waited with hugs and a belated birthday party.

"DeeDee" had been in three foster homes that first year but adapted well. One lingering symptom of her insecurity was she would clutch my left pant leg, clinging with all her might and following me everywhere. The most unsettling indication of her previous misfortunes was when I would move the furniture while vacuuming the living room, DeeDee would go to a corner, sit, and quietly sob. She had already had enough change to last a lifetime.

DeeDee was soon in love with her big sister. Suzie welcomed the new addition with excitement. The two soon became inseparable and settled into a lifelong friendship.

⁂

It is strange the things we remember.... One Easter we gave each of the girls a baby duck. Squeals of joy met the little fluffy yellow babies that morning, and the girls held them constantly while considering names for their new pets. It was a day or so later when they decided to take the baby ducks up into their tree house. DeeDee made the fatal mistake of thinking her *bird* could fly; she gently gave it a little shove off the ledge of the tree house floor—then watched in dismay as it plummeted to the ground, landing with a thud. The sweet, innocent fluff ball lay lifeless as both Suzie and DeeDee screamed at the top of their lungs. I rushed outside to utter confusion. The girls were trying to figure out what had gone wrong; DeeDee only wanted to help it fly.

A brief but very heartrending memorial service was held in our backyard that afternoon, and our conversation at the dinner table was about ducks' lack of ability to fly, and why.

⁂

Our little town held an annual festival. At this event, they held a community wide beauty pageant in which a junior and senior court was selected. When DeeDee was six years old, we entered her in the junior court selection, and she was chosen to be one of the princesses! Our daughter would represent our town in parades and celebrations, making appearances throughout our county during the summer.

On one particular day, DeeDee was to ride a float in her first appearance as a princess. Jeff had work to do; bales of hay needed to be put in the barn since rain was predicted for the next day. If the hay got wet it would reduce its selling price, so Jeff felt it was necessary for him to stay behind and get them protected.

As we prepared to leave, I lamented several times how much we would miss him and wished he would come with us. I even offered to help later; I could drive the truck while he loaded the bales of hay; then he could join us for the momentous event. After thinking a minute, Jeff smiled and agreed. We would work together through the night to secure the hay. He would finish the essential chores and be able to see the parade as well.

The afternoon made us both so proud. DeeDee was adorable on the float, waving to the onlookers. As the float passed us, we burst with pride. She could not have been more *our daughter*. Being adopted made no difference to us as her parents. She proved it was the same for her as she called, "Hi Mommy. Hi Daddy," before moving on down the street.

Later, we slipped into our work clothes at home, prepared to work into the night to get the hay into the barn. Working at a good pace, the girls were curled up in the truck cab beside me, sleeping soundly after the big day.

We had hauled several loads when the sky began to open up. My stomach knotted as the first sprinkles of rain hit the windshield; Jeff was getting angry. Minutes later he jumped into the truck so we could get what hay we had loaded to the barn quickly. I hurriedly drove to the barn in an attempt to give protection to the hay, but I was definitely not able to protect myself.

Jeff's scathing words began to tell me, in no uncertain terms, it was my fault we had just lost several hundred dollars' worth of sales. He reasoned, if I had not convinced him to go to the parade, if he had just stayed home, our hay would already have been stored when it began to rain. His humiliation of me continued; I was such a useless wife, not a helpmate but a waste and hindrance to everyone. I had heard it all before—and I was convinced I deserved every word of his verbal assault. I wondered if perhaps God created me as a joke; did He create me because someone needed a target or a punching bag? Jeff ranted on....

I had never seen my parents fight—**never**. I could tell when there was discord in the house, but any dispute was always settled privately. Since I had not been taught a method of diffusing arguments, I did the only things I knew to do: retreat, apologize, beg for forgiveness, and accept full responsibility. I truly believed I was responsible for the situation because of what Jeff called, "my lapses of judgment."

How could we be so blind? The answer for us (God's Word) lay within arm's reach at the head of our bed, or often was still riding around in the backseat of the car—but we ignored it.

Slowly I began to withdraw, never sure what I might say or do to bring on the next flare-up. During one particularly ugly argument, I found myself on the kitchen floor. I remember waking up with Jeff's face inches from mine, shaking me, and telling me I was faking unconsciousness—after his abuse had become physical and he had knocked me out. I have no idea how long I was oblivious to my surroundings.

◦◦◦◦◦◦◦

Another time I was told to have new tires put on our car. Given all the information, I was instructed to leave by ten o'clock in the morning so I would be home no later than one o'clock in the afternoon. Jeff would be home by then, and I was to be there when he arrived. For some reason I did not leave by the appointed time and found myself with a very narrow margin of time to complete my tasks and return. With the tires replaced, I sped for home to avoid any trouble. Then disaster struck. The front passenger tire fell off the rim. My car was dragging down the street on the drum. Once I safely pulled the car to a stop, I ran to a nearby house to call for help. Thankfully, the Les Schwab truck arrived in minutes.

Discovering the mechanics had not tightened the lug nuts properly, the technicians wanted to take the car back to the shop to correct the mistake. I knew I was already close to being late, so I begged them to just do the best they could and let me get home—it was vital. I was afraid the tire would come off again, but I was more afraid of what Jeff would do if I arrived home late.

I drove home as swiftly as I could. When the driveway came into view, my heart sank…. Jeff's car was already in the garage. I knew I was in for a challenging afternoon.

Angry words and accusations flew at me, along with questions as to why I had not left home at the appointed time. My explanations were not enough to calm Jeff's anger. He picked up his new watch from the kitchen table and threw it onto the sidewalk outside the back door, where it shattered into a million pieces. His shouting continued, "Why did you pretend to have a brain of your own? Why hadn't you done what you were told?" Crying and pleading for his forgiveness, I apologized as I gathered the broom and began to clean up the mess. The yelling continued, "See what you made me do? You did this! It was your fault. Do you enjoy upsetting me?"

With each occurrence of such outbursts, the void inside me grew larger, and the isolation deepened. Why was I ever born? What purpose did I serve?

﹡﹡﹡

There was only one incident from which I ever walked away. Jeff and I were working in tandem to clean up an area of the farm. On a steep hill of the property, I was driving the tractor while Jeff walked behind me to weed the areas the tractor blades could not reach. When Jeff would indicate for me to stop, the tractor would settle and roll back a bit because of the steep vertical incline. Gravity is not a force with which one can negotiate. If Jeff was not paying careful attention, he would be working in close proximity to the tractor, and the blades of the mechanism would come frighteningly near his legs. He began to accuse me of trying to get even with him, for the latest incident, by attempting to cut off his legs. After trying several times to get him to listen to reason, I got off the tractor and walked the several miles home. I was usually too afraid of the repercussions to challenge Jeff, but this time the circumstances were absolutely terrifying to me—wondering if the next time I had to stop, my horrible fear would be realized and Jeff would be seriously injured.

Since I was the boss's wife, Jeff expected that I should be the pacesetter— setting an example the hired farmhands could follow. If we were weeding in the berry rows, I was expected to be further down the row than the other workers—regardless of the plethora of weeds. Unreasonably, it did not matter if the water barrel was empty, and I took time off from weeding to fill it. It did not matter if a piece of equipment broke down, and I had to take time to get it fixed or replaced. It did not matter if I had to go to the bathroom. I was expected to have superhero strength, speed, and stamina. All of these chores had to be done, and I would be in trouble if they were not, but I also had to be ahead of everyone else in the regular functions of the farm. I needed to be Super Woman, and I was not good enough.

There were some good times, despite the anger. We became ardent coin collectors, loved clamming and hunting and had some wonderful holidays. There were fantastic annual family camping beach trips with parents, aunts, uncles, and cousins. There were quiet times, too, which were memorable. Jeff could be so tender, so compassionate; it was as though I was living with two different men. The problem was I could never be sure which man would be present: the man who promised to love and honor me, or the man waiting for me to do something "stupid" so he could "justifiably" put me in my place.

Our difficulties were not entirely Jeff's fault either. I was too immature to deal with such temper and violence. I perpetuated things I perhaps could have stopped. I could have stood up to Jeff. I could have acknowledged his temper was uncontrollable and attempted to get him help. I could have sought help for myself. Instead, I accepted what I was told: all of it was my responsibility and my fault.

Although I believe Jeff wished he had control of his temper, the unfortunate truth is his temper wounded everyone involved. I was anything but happy, and the girls were sandwiched between an insecure and immobile mother and a frightful father. Jeff never physically abused the girls; he absolutely adored them. Still, the psychological effects of both of our actions were certainly wounding them: two immature girls (about eight years old and eleven years old), doing what they knew to do in those situations of disparity, trying to find answers. Many times I packed a suitcase and loaded the girls in the car, intending to leave. After driving around for a couple hours, predictably, I would arrive back home.

God's Word says, *"Ask and it will be given to you; seek and you will find; knock and the door will be opened to you"* (Matthew 7:7). Jeff and I sought solutions but chose worldly answers, which only drew us deeper into the mire. We found other paths, and like the Prodigal Son of Matthew 14, we eagerly took them. Our marriage continued to deteriorate, leading to what would be a disastrous ending for us all.

⁂

For some unremembered reason, once again, Jeff and I began to fight. Suzie and DeeDee recognized the signs. Usually they went rapidly to their rooms, shut the doors, and turned on anything to block out the shouting. This time Suzie uncharacteristically stayed in the family room. After a shouting contest and a shoving match, Jeff stormed from the room. I believed the worst was over. He would watch TV, and I would retreat to the bedroom.

Instead, Jeff returned—with an axe in his hand! He began to pursue me through the house. I was screaming at the top of my lungs when Suzie suddenly emerged from the family room. Compelled by some unseen resource, Suzie stepped directly into the path of her father declaring, "If you get Mom with that axe, you will have to go through me!"

The next moments seemed to move in slow motion: Jeff released the axe, and it hit the floor. Shaking his head, he left the room without a word. Suzie stood alone; her body shaking uncontrollably, silently, with tears rushing down her pale, drawn face. I clutched her to me and tried to reassure her everything would be fine, even while emphatically telling her to never again challenge her father in a time of rage. I squeezed her so tightly she had to pull away to breathe.

That incident served as a wake-up call for me! It was one thing for me to pay the costly price of Jeff's violence, however, for my preteen daughter to face that kind of violent behavior was intolerable. I knew something would have to change soon, or there would be calamitous consequences. The drama was finished for that night, but there would be many more incidents, each ending with me apologizing for starting the fight—for being born a mistake.

I remember one day looking out the kitchen window and thinking, *I can't do this for the rest of my life. I'm not going to last. Even worse, what about the girls?* I knew Jeff loved them, but when his temper flared, anger was the ultimate power that needed to be fed and satisfied. What I wanted to be a fairy-tale marriage had become an out-of-control nightmare. I desperately wanted this marriage to work, so did Jeff. The problem was neither of us knew how to change the anger that was obviously destroying it.

Chapter Three

During the sixteenth year of our marriage, I stepped into a totally new, uncharted territory, a far cry from what I had known. It was a place where I became a stranger even to myself. The future could have been so different; what happened could have been avoided....

About this time we began to socialize with a different group of friends than before. In addition to working the farm, Jeff had taken a second job; our social life began to expand. We were invited to picnics and parties—a welcome break from Saturday night fighting at home. We became especially close to one particular couple, Gary and Liz. Jeff and Gary had met at their workplace and the friendship grew during our social outings.

At the parties we attended, I had the feeling someone was watching me. When I gazed around, I saw Gary across the room smiling a huge smile at me. My heart leapt; could it be possible there was a man who thought I was appealing? A man who thought I had significance? Maybe, just maybe, could it be possible Jeff was wrong about me being worthless? It was gratifying to hope someone in the world saw something in me, however small, which called him to recognize me. I soon began returning a second look or a smile back at Gary. There was no law against a smile, or the light brush of his presence as he walked by, was there?

Sin is like fishing: Bait entices us. We talk ourselves into believing our actions are harmless. "Nibbles" lead to "samples," which leads to "testing the waters." When we enjoy the results, we take bigger and bigger bites of the bait. Slowly we slide ever deeper into a deceptive security as we play with the temptation, justifying our seemingly innocent actions. We become genuinely hooked as we take bigger bites, enjoying the newfound pleasure. We think we control the bait, but sooner or later, the bait controls us. Almost imperceptibly, we discover ourselves consumed by the thrill—the acceptance. The emptiness we have carried inside for so long, cries out for more and more.

Somewhere down the road, however, there is a price to be paid. Like the fish who took the bait, we too, now find ourselves in the frying pan. Reflecting on what we have done leaves us with guilt, shame, low self-esteem, crushed dreams, and fear of exposure. There is no time limit, but we cannot wave a fist in God's face without reaping repercussions.

Gary was not particularly handsome; Jeff would have won a contest between them, hands down. Adultery is not about nice clothes, a higher education, or a better financial situation. It has nothing to do with social standings, stability, or personalities. It is all about *feelings*—and I felt alive again! For the first time in years, when I looked into a man's eyes—Gary's eyes—I saw myself as pretty, desirable...maybe even smart. I was a person of real value with something worthwhile to offer—and I was absolutely starved for attention and admiration.

Calls began; after all, we were friends. *Coincidently,* the calls always occurred when Jeff was away at work. At first they were innocent enough, and it seemed like we could converse endlessly—the way Jeff and I once had been able to talk. Gary and I talked about the news, our kids, movies, and he always expressed value for my opinion. At times, he would ask for my thoughts when I did not express them.

Without realizing it, I began to anxiously await Gary's calls, which were now daily and predictable. With the fledgling growth of my self-esteem, I started taking more time with my hair and applied a little makeup, even when I was not going anywhere. Passing by a mirror, a quick glance reflected a different woman than the one who had previously stared back. I could see a difference from deep inside, even when I was not wearing makeup.

Then came an invitation for a cup of coffee. What possible harm could come from a cup of coffee? He wanted my opinion on a situation arising between him and Liz. Who better to turn to than a good friend—to get *her* perspective? We were just friends who had a lot in common, and he was seeking my help. With every step, I found justification. But deep within, I knew I was kidding myself about the real reason I was meeting Gary.

The meetings soon escalated to out-of-the-way places where we were sure we would not be interrupted. I made excuses to leave home, and when I returned, I lied about where I had been and what I had done. After all, I reasoned, Jeff would never understand how Gary and I could have so much in common, be such good friends, and yet still be innocent.

There were times when Jeff would stumble onto a part of my story that did not quite make sense. "Are you saying I am lying?" I would challenge arrogantly. Jeff's suspicions grew as my loyalties began to wane, and my interests changed. Life was no longer about housework, meals, and being a good wife. I now lived life in a sense of anticipation; I counted the hours, minutes, and seconds until the next call or coffee.

Strangely enough, Jeff's temper seemed to simultaneously wane. I began to feel, for the first time in a very, very, long time, I was in control of my life. Jeff seemed almost afraid of me, or at least afraid of what he thought I might do. Sadly, I relished every moment.

One day I mentioned to Gary that Jeff had a meeting the following night and would not be home until late. The next night Jeff was not yet home, but as I headed for bed, there was a knock at the door. I opened the door, and there he was—Gary. He stepped across the threshold, smiled, and explained he had run out to get some cough syrup for his kids and thought he would stop by. We both knew my house was miles out of his way, yet he came. He told me how beautiful I looked in my light-blue housecoat, and even with my hair in disarray, how sexy I looked. My heart raced at the thought. Gary stayed only a minute, but as he left, he embraced me, kissed me passionately, then turned and left without another word, closing the door behind him.

I stood there unseeing, my heart beating so loudly I was afraid it would wake the girls. I had not felt so alive in years. I was overwhelmed, totally consumed with my newly entrenched value and with the physical emotions that had been aroused by Gary's visit. Just the touch of his hand sent shivers of ecstasy through my body. The emptiness inside me was gone. I had significance! Suddenly, I believed I had something that was important enough to offer to someone else. I believed I had someone who would appreciate my contributions to the relationship. The stark contrast to what I was accustomed to with Jeff was like a super strong magnet; I was incapable of resisting the attraction.

The movie playing in my mind was interrupted by the airline attendant asking if I would like a snack or drink. I shook my head "no" and prayed the interruption would not stop the playback of my past. God was exposing things of which I needed to be conscious. So I closed my eyes again, and waited for the show to restart....

Unrelentingly and predictably, the emotions between Gary and I accelerated as my marriage deteriorated. The old adage is true: What you put time and effort into will be the thing that thrives and flourishes. Regardless of obstacles, Gary and I would make it to our secret rendezvous, which never seemed to last long enough. We would soon have to return to our own spouses and the humdrum of our lives. Our greatest aspiration was to spend an entire day together, unhampered by the clock.

We got the chance for that uninterrupted day. Gary announced that Liz was planning to take the children to see her parents, and the drive and visit would take the entire day. Imagine—a whole day! If we were going to have this great day, our first real time together, I wanted it to be extra special. I decided we would have a picnic, and packed a wonderful lunch of sandwiches, grapes, cheesecake, and wine.

Always cautious to not be seen, we drove to an area we did not frequent. No one who knew us would see us. It was a beautiful summer day: blue skies, a few white fluffy clouds, green grass, and birds singing. We enjoyed the food, each other's company, and a leisurely stroll along the edge of a river, arm in arm, hand in hand. It was unlike anything I had experienced in my life. I was not hampered by fear. Walking by his side, I felt like someone very special as he took deliberate care of me. I spent an entire day in a secure, emotional bliss. Soon I felt it would be like this for the rest of my lifetime.

⸙

I remember late one night I had planned to meet Gary after the girls were asleep. Arriving home earlier than Jeff's normal schedule, I was taken aback when I found him in the kitchen— waiting. "Where have you been?" was his reasonable question.

"Just wanted to get away for a while. Drove around, that's all," was my snide response. I was known to hop in the car and drive for miles when I was upset or angry. Jeff simply did not believe me; it was evident by the look in his eyes. An unmistakable look of concern and hurt crossed his face; he knew better. But I blew it off. So what! What was happening was more important for me, more valuable than his anguish.

Sin always has a season of enjoyment as we are drawn into its web. After years of abuse, I *believed* I had found someone who loved me just for me. The emotional ecstasy filled my emptiness with all the things I had so longed for, and it felt wonderful. Thoughts of breaking up two families, and destroying the worlds of five children, seemed inconsequential in comparison to the happiness I had found. I was in desperate need of confirmation. I was a legitimate human being; God had *not* designed me as a punching bag *nor* as a joke. Gary made it clear I was the most important person in his world, and I was validated as an individual. Selfishly, I gladly and willingly grasped at his answer, trying to make myself whole again.

Gary assured me Liz had never really understood him, and they had never had a happy marriage. As the Prodigal Son heard the beckoning call of all the wonders the world had to offer, so did I. There was no contemplation of consequences as I expectantly plotted this new life. Gary and I spent time together as often as possible, sometimes in parks, sometimes in motels, or occasionally a few brief moments in a store or restaurant. The encounters never seemed to come often enough, and always seemed to end too soon.

Although God, as always, was waiting, I did not invite Him to be a part of my life and my decisions. The only reason I ever called to Him was when I really needed help with a situation I could not control. Perhaps the reason I did not call on Him at other times was because I knew what His response would be—and I did not want to give up my happiness. It was all about me.

How easily an attitude can be adopted, becoming a dangerous habit that leads us to do and be all kinds of things of which we never dreamed we were capable. I believed I had all the answers. I did not need God to tell me I was now a complete person; I already knew it!

What we were doing was wrong; but it felt so right!! God says we should not base our actions on our human feelings but trust Him to guide our paths. I knew this, but at the time, it was not pertinent. Nothing else mattered but the love I had found.

Chapter Four

I told myself Jeff would be relieved to get rid of me; his worthless wife would be gone. The girls would no longer be witnesses to the physical and verbal abuse. My marriage was beyond repairing, and I now had a new direction in which to move. I was now going to begin living my life. Finally! I deserved it; everyone deserves to be happy. At what cost? We will make it work, just watch! Everyone will be better off. The girls would not bear witness to fighting and would have a happy mom. For me, happiness of which I had only dreamed awaited. For Gary, a wife whom he loved, and one who loved him, adored him, and understood him as no one else ever had.

For months Gary and I lived in a snare of denials and lies. The conjured up lies had a way of building on each other and becoming more and more complex. Because the *experiences* we were inventing did not really happen, it was difficult to keep the details of our stories straight. The web of lies threatened to entangle us as our spouses detected contradicting details. Not only our spouses, other people too were beginning to get more and more suspicious. We had to do something.

Gary and I began discussing how to shape our shared future. Because we had mutual friends, we wanted to save face. After discussing options in great detail, the constant verbal abuse and threat of domestic violence I was experiencing made it easy to decide I would be the first to leave. Gary would stay with Liz a few months longer before he, too, would announce he wanted a divorce. Hopefully the gap of time between the separations from our spouses would seem less suspicious and no one would connect the dots.

There would also be the added benefit of not having to work around so many schedules. I no longer would have to keep track of where Jeff was and when he would be home. The girls were old enough I could leave them alone for a few minutes to run to "the grocery store." When Gary would call, I could easily slip out for a short rendezvous—and more frequently.

I began to prepare to move to a neighboring town, taking the girls and telling the world I wanted a divorce. I would be the first ever in my family to do so. The stigma attached to the word "divorce" made me believe my friends would be repulsed. Jeff continually perpetuated the thought that no one would value my friendship.

The Saturday morning we sat the girls down at the kitchen table is etched forever in my memory. The words stumbled out of my mouth: "Dad and I are getting a d-divorce. We both love you, but we won't be living together anymore. I am taking an apartment in Brookside, and we'll be moved before your new school starts." I paused and waited.

The silence was deadening. I am not sure what I had expected, but at least I anticipated someone to say something. Suzie finally spoke. "Well, at least we won't have to hear you fighting anymore." DeeDee just sat, no verbal response, her blue eyes wide and filled with tears tumbling down onto her face. It almost seemed as though she had been able to remove herself from it all.

I made no formal announcement; I just disappeared. I prepared my life as I needed. I found a job in the floral business (because I had worked in several shops, I was already well known), which fit the hours when the girls were at school. Quietly, we moved into an apartment—a nicer domicile than the farmhouse we had called home. Jeff helped us move into our own apartment—probably thinking I might change my mind if he was cooperative. Getting the girls' records and signing them up for their new schools, I found little time for anything else. Keeping busy made the loneliness of not seeing Gary easier too. I pacified myself by thinking it was only temporary. Once I was settled, we had a lifetime ahead of us.

The real victims in divorce are the innocent children. Psychologists tell us in a divorce, children usually blame themselves for the split. Whether acknowledged or not, they carry a burden of guilt for the wreckage. As time passed, Jeff and I played a game common for divorced couples: The game of *favorite parent* trying to outdo each other. It is a game with far-reaching results on the children involved—and nobody ever wins.

⁂

To his credit, Jeff tried hard to pull back together the shattered pieces of our family that resulted from my actions. He took us all to Hawaii for ten days, to just get away with no *distractions*, in hopes it would rebuild his family, which was slipping away. The dilemma is that both spouses must be willing to bring the family back together, and in our case, the problem did not add up mathematically: two minus one, a couple does not make.

I could scarcely wait to get back to my new life and made no effort to restore our family during those few days in paradise. I wonder if I had put the same effort into saving my marriage as I put into the affair, might it have been saved.

⁂

At the vacation's end, I arrived at my apartment to discover a gigantic yellow ribbon attached to my front door. The song "Tie a Yellow Ribbon" was popular, and it referred to putting a ribbon around a tree to indicate the occupant was still loved after being gone. I understood the implications of the welcome message; my heart jumped. Scurrying to the phone as soon as I could get a minute alone, I reassured Gary I was home to stay.

It was not long before I began to realize the repercussions of my divorce. It rarely ends amiably and always extracts personal costs from everyone concerned.

It is like pouring a drop of black paint into a can of white paint, stirring it a few times, then changing your mind and trying to remove the black from the white. It just does not happen. Two brought together in body, spirit, and soul can never be completely separate again.

Jeff and I had promised before God to love, honor, and obey until death parted us. But it was not death that brought about the divorce; it was me and my new love—yet I would deny this for many years.

The girls and I launched our new lives in our new surroundings all alone. We were settled in by September when the girls began school. They seemed to adapt easily and made good friends. An unexpected opportunity for some spending money presented itself when the manager of our apartment complex asked them to keep the laundry room clean. Gary intended to leave Liz the coming spring and move in with a coworker. We had it all planned; but plans do not always work as expected, or do they?

Suzie, DeeDee, and I all thrived on life in the city. Unlike living in the country, my teenaged girls enjoyed the experience of being able to visit their friends who lived nearby. I loved the freedom of not being blamed for everything that happened. Burning the cake was not a federal offense for which I should be punished.

One day it rained, and I stood smiling, eyes closed, feeling raindrops hit my face, knowing this time there would be no accusations to worry about. If the hay got wet, it would not be my fault. I knew now when I made a mistake, I could fix it. If the food was not salted enough, a salt shaker could be placed on the table.

I was no longer being told I was too stupid to keep a household. In addition, I loved my new job, and the salary was sufficient to meet the bills.

The biggest advantage I found was that my time was my own. I could come home from work late or go out to dinner. No one would yell at me or accuse me, whether it was justified or not. The peace was like water to a thirsty plant; I could grow and bloom in my own way without criticism or intimidation. Indeed, like the Prodigal Son, I believed I was now master of my own destiny; it felt fantastic.

⁂

I received some vindication. Within just a few weeks of my leaving, Jeff called in a dither because he could not figure out how to process the bills or balance the farm books. This had previously been solely my responsibility. Jeff asked if I would teach him how to work on the finances and show him the systems and shortcuts I had developed over the years. He came to my apartment. A few hours later, he left with three stacks of bills: one to pay, another to talk about with proprietors and make arrangements, and a third to be held for additional information.

After Jeff had gone, I sat at the table with the sudden realization I was not so dumb; he was the one who needed help. Maybe I was not as useless, or as much of a hindrance, as he had led me to believe for years. I smiled with contentment.

⁂

Jeff would take the girls every other weekend, picking them up after work between five and six o'clock. I noticed he now carried a pack of cigarettes; he had never smoked while we were married. Occasionally, Jeff would not arrive until later in the evening, and sometimes he had the smell of liquor on his breath. This was very out of character for the man I once knew. My refusal to let Jeff take Suzie and DeeDee when he had been drinking too much only made him more aggravated, but I felt I needed to protect the girls.

I may have been aware of the undercurrents of pain, but I was not willing to acknowledge Jeff was hurting from losing his family. The smoking and drinking were only efforts to ease the pain he was experiencing. Neither would I accept any guilt because of his pain. I told myself, *let him hurt.* I'm the good parent who removed Suzie, DeeDee, and I from an unhealthy environment. He was getting what I thought he deserved.

Oh how I deceived myself! A lie spoken often enough soon seems like the truth. I believed my own lies and justified every bit of my sinful behavior. What I failed to remember while justifying my behavior to make myself feel better, is God sees it all. Even the craftiest among men cannot hide their disobedience from Him—and neither could I.

On the weekends when the girls were gone, I made plans for my evenings too. I would meet up with Gary somewhere, or when he could slip away from Liz, he would come to the apartment.

At Christmas, Gary was still with Liz and their children. That Christmas was one of the loneliest holidays I have ever celebrated. I generously allowed Jeff to have the girls for a few hours, and I spent most of the day alone. Gary was able to slip away Christmas night for a couple hours. Again, he pledged his devotion to me was immeasurable, now and forever. In the brilliance of his promise, the shadows of the lonely hours dimmed. It was worth it.

Through it all, I continued to regularly attend church, say all the right things, and let everyone know I was, indeed, a Christian. God's Word was evidence! After all, it sat prestigiously at the head of my bed. Further proof was the beautiful scripture in the gold frame that hung in the front hall. I prayed most of the time before meals and even put money into the offering (if I had any extra). God was good, and so was my life—as long as I could run it my way.

Gary began divorce proceedings within days of moving out in March. It was natural for him to visit us at the apartment as an old friend. He gave the girls extra attention as we went on picnics, attended carnivals, or stayed home and watched movies. He even cooked some very tasty meals. Like we were assembling a puzzle, we began carefully putting pieces together to begin building what we thought would be the flawless picture of our new family.

Gary was getting along well with the girls. Our one concern was they might find him in the house late at night and ruin our "only friends" image. To ensure our continued successful deception, we devised a signal: if the porch light was off, he was unable to visit; light on—all clear. Leaving the patio door unlocked made it easy for Gary to come in unannounced. The ease with which we accomplished our ruse sucked us further into arrogance, making us feel even more in control of our situation, emotions, and destiny. Slowly, we integrated the idea of a blended family and high hopes for having a new dad.

Gary and I continued planning our future, including a new home. We found a house the girls and I loved, much better than the one we left behind along with my marriage. At the farmhouse, the girls would sometimes awake to find bats on their bedroom ceiling. While Jeff had never felt it a threat, the girls disagreed; they would even sleep with their heads under the covers.

A call from the realtor informed us an offer had been made by another buyer on our potential house. If we were serious about buying it, we needed to place a better offer before the end of the day. Gary was out of town; we had a hurried telephone conference. Immediately after work I signed a full offer on what would become our new home. The girls squealed with joy from their excitement.

Even though Gary's name could not appear on the title (he was still legally married to Liz), he proved to me he was invested in our future by providing a portion of the funds for the down payment. Some of my friends had said the marriage would never happen, but any doubts about my upcoming marriage and new life dissipated. Gary and I had a home in which to begin our lifetime together, and all my fears were silenced. The girls and I moved into the house two weeks before the wedding.

While my marriage to Jeff had been a grandeur event, with all my family and friends in attendance, this wedding would be small, with just a few friends attending. We invited his three children. Their mother encouraged them to attend their father's wedding, but they all declined the offer. I was disappointed. I had dreams of a blended family consisting of my children, his children, and hopefully our children, but Gary's sons never truly accepted me.

Appearance was very important to us, so our guests were mostly newer acquaintances who would not question our timing or past actions. Two days after Gary's divorce was final, we were married. Again, I had forgotten God sees it all, and He was very aware of everything that precipitated my second marriage.

My sister stayed with the girls while Gary and I celebrated our honeymoon night at a beautiful local hotel. When I entered the room, it was filled with the sweet fragrance of gardenias, my favorite flower. A large crystal bowl, filled with floating gardenias, had been placed prominently on the table. Beside the bowl was a note from Gary, affirming his love and our unlimited future together. I was sure nothing but happiness and joy lay ahead.

I had everything I wanted: my girls, a new home, a husband who really loved me, and a great job as well. How could I have regrets when life had become so complete? I could never remember feeling so whole, and this new life was all mine.

One night shortly after our marriage, we hosted a party and the girls had friends stay overnight. During the evening, the group of teens disappeared for a short time and later surfaced in our family room, devious smiles on their faces. "Hey, Mom! Dad! Go check out your car."

We all headed for the driveway to find the car jam-packed with crushed newspapers and "Congratulations" written in whipped cream. Everyone laughed, and then the whole story was revealed.

The girls, wanting to maintain some wedding traditions, had gone door-to-door telling our new neighbors, "Our mom and dad just got married. We want to fix up their car. Can you help?" The neighbors pitched in, and I looked around to see many of those neighbors watching from their doorways. It was a Kodak moment, to say the least.

⚜

Life just kept getting better and better. I had worked as a florist for the past ten years, dreaming of someday owning my own shop. My wish came true with the opportunity to purchase a shop of my own. Rechristened as the Full Bloom, I added the prestige of being a shop owner to the joy of a new husband, a new home, and freedom like I had never experienced before.

After only two years, the excitement we experienced upon the purchase of our first mingled home diminished. We had an opportunity to trade it for what I dubbed my *dream home.* It was pure perfection, with the added benefit of being much closer to the flower shop. My life was like a dream, yet even better, for I knew eventually dreams end. Gary and I pledged to each other this marriage was "until death do us part;" ours would last for a lifetime. Little did I know what was ahead was about as far as possible from the *happily ever after* I envisioned. Instead, a nightmare was on the horizon where I would harvest what I had sown.

Sorrow

Chapter Five

I settled into my newly married status, but I began to notice little things in Gary's behavior I had previously been too infatuated to see. Certainly I had been aware that Gary drank; one of the places we would frequently rendezvous was an out-of-the-way bar. I had not been aware how frequent or excessive his drinking had become, because he was always in control. I guess I was naïve. I always thought an alcoholic was a person who required certain levels of alcohol in their blood stream constantly. Wrong!

We had a pool table and all his buddies from work began to drop by after work for a game or two. It began unexpectedly and then became the norm. In addition, they anticipated large quantities of beer would accompany the pool games. I felt very uncomfortable with the amount of drinking taking place, especially around my daughters. But Gary reminded me they were *his* friends, and I was to back off! I redefined my definition of an alcoholic to include someone who cannot stop drinking once they start. Gary was not drunk every day, but the alcohol controlled him as soon as he took the first drink.

One Fourth of July, we attended a cul-de-sac holiday picnic where there was a considerable amount of alcohol flowing freely. As the party wore on, the variety of choices shrunk. So Gary volunteered to go purchase more alcohol. I asked him not to drive since he had already been drinking. He pushed me aside with a few choice words to punctuate the action and drove away. On his return, I begged him not to drink anymore and to refrain from returning to the party. With one swift motion of his hand, I found myself on our kitchen floor and blood streaming from my mouth. It was the first, and last, time he ever physically struck me. I gave him an ultimatum; I knew I no longer had to be anyone's punching bag. "Hit me again and you are history!" I screamed. It was the first time I can remember standing my ground, and I recall being proud of myself. He threw a sneer in my direction and returned to the party alone, arriving home much later that night. The incident was never spoken of again.

As with the Prodigal Son, I would soon find myself lamenting over the condition of my marriage, and why it was that way. The big question would always end up: What do I do now? I had believed I was currently in a safe and secure marriage. However, I found I was, again, being physically and emotionally abused. I thought this marriage would be better than the one from which I walked away. My dreams of a perfect, blended family were far from the reality of what I was living.

⨈⨈⨈⨈⨈⨈⨈

Gary's boys never really received me. At the time I was so blinded I could not understand why. When it was our weekend to have them, he would spend money like water through a sieve to show them a good time. Whether it was a symptom of guilt or of trying to buy their affections, I was never sure.

To finance those weekends, Suzie, DeeDee, and I would go without. No, we never went without any of life's necessities, but Gary would always want to wait for the fun family activities. Only when the boys were with us, would we go out to dinner, go to the movies, go roller skating, or buy the boys a remote controlled airplane or other such bribes. Whatever their little fingers pointed out, it seemed to become theirs in the blink of an eye. Suzie and DeeDee noticed but never challenged him about it. I think they understood it was the same game and rules they had seen Jeff and me playing. They knew it was not about the explicit actions of buying the gifts, but about the implicit insecure feelings created as a result of the divorce.

I chuckle to this day about a Friday night when Gary arrived home rather late. Although their father was not yet there, the boys arrived. My prepared meal was nothing they especially liked, which only included all meat pizzas, Hawaiian pizzas, or Burger King.

After dinner we all moved into the family room for an evening of TV. On this particular night, there were no special rentals or a night of lavish spending out on the town. Shortly after realizing this, one of the boys began complaining about his stomach, he added he might be getting the flu. "I need to call Mom and just go home."

The look Suzie gave me, and I returned, indicated there was no flu, he was just not being entertained in the manner he had come to expect. Suzie impishly suggested, "We have some Pepto-Bismol in the bathroom, which might help ease the discomfort." As she said it, neither of us could look at each other, and we could hardly keep a straight face.

His response was predictable, "No, I just need to go home! That stuff tastes awful."

"Oh," I replied with an air of assurance, "I am sure Pepto-Bismol will take care of it. At the very least, it would be a great precaution. No need for you to go home; your dad would miss seeing you later." I insisted on his taking the vile pink liquid and comforted him, "Soon, you will feel better. If not, we will try an additional dosage."

Curiously enough, the one dose was all it took; he was cured. Gary arrived home later, and it went back to a typical weekend visit. Nevertheless, Suzie and I snicker about the episode even today.

To my dismay, I was beginning to realize this marriage was not the dream I had anticipated. I could not hide my sins; God is omnipresent...with me—and you—everywhere and all the time. I had deceived myself, believing I could get away with all my previous actions without repercussions. Gary and I had unwittingly positioned our marriage for trouble—and it would not be long before it showed itself.

Chapter Six

It was Mother's Day and we planned to attend church. Gary had been in one of his sulky moods and refused to accompany us. Returning home, I found him watching TV. As we entered the room, he grumbled something like, "Here you go. Now you can't play the *poor-me* bit." With that, he threw a brown bag across the room at me. Inside was the ugliest housecoat you can visualize. It was multi-colored, striped, five sizes too large, and the price tag—clearly hanging from the sleeve—had been reduced twice on the clearance rack. I never wore the housecoat that would have put Joseph's treasured, multi-colored coat to shame. It hung in my closet, reminding me of just another failure in the perfect life I had crafted.

I excitedly looked forward to my birthday, but my special day came and went and nothing. It was two days later when I tearfully built up the courage to ask Gary if he forgot it; his response was, "I knew. I don't care about your birthday, not now or ever." My heart burst into pieces as if it had been trampled by a herd of wild horses. I hurriedly exited the room to conceal the sobs that leapt from the depths of my soul. I firmly resolved not to grant him the privilege of seeing how effectively he had hurt me. Even a simple "Happy Birthday" would have helped to ease the feelings of abandonment I was experiencing, but it was becoming abundantly clear: He did not care. Not now—not ever.

Ordinary days could be every bit as painful as well. Yet there is something about Christmas, birthdays, anniversaries—those special days around which you build hope in making treasured memories to last for a lifetime—that seem to remain in memory as the most agonizing when they are scarred. By my own choices, I had become the Prodigal Daughter. I began to catch a slight glimpse of the consequences and the depth of pain the Prodigal Son must have experienced.

It had snowed all day. The ground had accumulated several inches already, and I dreaded the drive home. On the evening news, the weatherman already promised more of the same snowy conditions through the night, making the morning commute even more treacherous. The snow was beautiful, and the pure white flakes seemed to make everything so fresh and clean. Yet, at the same time, it made navigating the roads a nightmare.

Arriving home, I began to prepare supper. I chatted with Gary over a sizzling skillet, explaining to him I was really terrified of driving back to work the following day. I was even so bold as to suggest maybe he could drive me. He could leave a little early and drop me off. I would even be very happy to wait at the shop the extra hour until he got off, if it meant not driving on those horrendous roads. I was caught completely off guard when he hesitatingly announced that he had already offered to help one of his fellow employees. *She* was really counting on him to pick her up and transport her in the morning. I would need to find another way to work myself. "Besides," he added unsympathetically, "there is no need for anyone to baby you." I can still feel the ache that rose up in me at his callous attitude. Once again, I appeared to not have enough value to be worried about, even by my husband. It was only one of the times I faced that situation with Gary.

One Friday, I was driving home from Full Bloom. I watched as the signal light turned from red to green and proceeded into the intersection. Out of nowhere a sky-blue car whipped through his red light, scarcely missing me as I stomped down hard on my brakes with both feet. Although there was no physical damage done, when I arrived home a few minutes later, I was still trembling and emotionally upset. I tried to work through my fears by sharing the incident with my husband. He barely even acknowledged me as he perused the day's *important* events in the newspaper. Reflecting upon the episode for a minute, I sat down on the brown leather chair and asked him, "What would you do if I had been killed?"

Gary finally lowered the newspaper. He looked directly at me and, being in one of his dark moods, said without flinching, "Well, I'd take the day off, but would probably just go fishing. Doubt if I'd bother to make it to the service."

At first I thought he was trying to be funny, but as he raised the paper in front of him and resumed reading, it was absolutely clear he meant it. His wife's death, *my* death, would only be an excuse to go fishing! He would not have even bothered to pretend he was in mourning. I would never have said such a hurtful thing to a total stranger or even an enemy. How could he possibly say it about, and directly to, his wife—*me*?

There are times when I wish I could have seen into the future. But God, with all His insight, withholds that from His children. He has written into His Word His guidelines for life as well as the consequences; we just have to study the Bible for the knowledge and wisdom hidden within. I thought I was experiencing some of the worst possible moments in my lifetime. Not even close! My troubled marriage was about to get worse.

Suzie came to me and confided, "One late night when Gary had been drinking, he snuck into my room and touched me...um—inappropriately."

I watched her face as the room began to spin, the nausea rising from deep within my stomach, my throat swelling and tightening. No! He could not have done that! He promised to be a daddy to the girls! I clung to the sturdy door frame long enough to catch my breath, then continued leaning against it to help me remain standing. I debated the situation. Suzie's attitude lately had been defiant, at best; her latest boyfriend had recently been banned from our home because of his drug use. I sat for a long minute before I responded. "You are only saying it to upset me. Gary would never stoop so low! You want to hurt me, and I won't let you. He would never do such a thing. You and I haven't been getting along, but this is no way to get even. This is not funny!"

Like so many parents before me, I did not see the signs that were before me. Suzie had been withdrawing from Gary's presence and did not want to be left alone with him. Her rebellious attitude was starkly different from the helpful young lady she had been. I was too involved in my own problems to notice my daughter's.

Then I compounded the injury to her. Instead of asking more questions and investigating further, I immediately took my mate's side. She had confided in me, and I shut her down. It broke the fragile trust she had in our mother-daughter relationship. It could not have been easy coming to me with this sensitive and distasteful information. In less than five minutes, I left her unable to trust me and unsure of where to turn, either at that time or in the future.

In a split second, I was positive that God was out to punish me. Being a strong-headed, obstinate German, I determined I was on my own. I began believing the saying, "If it is to be, it is up to me." I could not count on anyone, not even my Creator. Not once in any of the situations in which I found myself, did it occur to me that He had not been able to rely on me. In retrospect, I have often wondered how many tears He shed, as my Father, when He watched me collapse under the burdens of my own making.

Suzie never repeated the allegation again. Yet years later, her claim would be validated when DeeDee admitted she had also been subject to one inappropriate encounter with Gary.

I have deeply regretted my own inaction about the accusations. Until proven false, any such revelation deserves to be—*and must* be, investigated. We are commanded to protect our children, especially when the protection is from our own family. I should have taken her side, without question, until there was resolution. Suzie should have been protected! Yet again, I had failed miserably. What kind of mother was I? Did I not remember my own mother's disbelief when I told her about Jeff's abuse, and how she just dismissed my feelings to a traumatic event in my life? I was now repeating her behaviors with my own children. I was too absorbed in my own life, and I had unknowingly placed my own needs above those of Suzie and DeeDee.

Chapter Seven

The flower shop had blossomed, no pun intended, and proved to be a wonderful investment! The floral wire service, which tracks the activities of all the local floral shops, declared the volume of business we conducted within the walls of our shop had made Full Bloom the number two florist in the community...up from number seven! Considering there were only seven floral shops in the community, it was quite the accomplishment.

As well as giving me a feeling of security, the shop had given me my own individuality. I had become well-known in the local florists' circle and the recognition gave me an identity I had never had before. This successful growth was the result of a lot of personal dedication and was at the great cost of time with my family. My life had many flaws, to say the least, but as my homelife deteriorated, I drew my sense of worth from the shop.

So much of myself was buried in the daily business of the shop; it was easy to ignore the clues my body was giving me, which said I was not feeling my best. I explained symptoms away and procrastinated about seeking medical help. Eventually, however, the "warning signs" could no longer go unnoticed. I broke down and set up an appointment with a doctor. I thought, a quick exam, some pills or a shot, and I will go merrily on my way. I was sure it was only a long-lasting and stubborn flu.

The day of my appointment arrived and I trudged off to see the doctor. After the examination, he delivered his diagnosis to me: I was pregnant. I laughingly explained to him he had to be mistaken. I had been told years before by another doctor I could not get pregnant! We had even adopted our second daughter, DeeDee, because of my inability to conceive. That was years ago. *Besides,* I mused, *what am I going to do with a baby at this stage in my life? I have a business to run! I have two girls who are almost grown. How would a baby affect my life? What would the introduction of a baby do to my marriage?* As I refocused my eyes on the doctor again, it was apparent he was not teasing me.

The aide, who had been standing quietly in the corner to monitor the examination process, suddenly broke her silence and made a remark that would alter my life forever. "Well, lucky for you, you don't have to do this; nowadays you have a choice."

"Choice!" What did she mean? As she continued the exchange, she assured me it was still *just tissue* but only if we dealt with the *problem* right away. It could be taken care of in two trouble-free appointments. I could move on with my life as if I had never encountered this problem. Her final promise, "You will never have to think about it again," still haunts me today. With my hard-won wisdom of retrospect, it seems strange. I was calling an innocent life a "problem" all because it did not fit into the selfish plan I had for my life.

Like Eve, who picked the forbidden fruit shown to her by the serpent in the Garden of Eden and offered it to her mate, Adam, I plucked the idea the nurse had shown me and rushed home to share it with Gary. Abortion was legal after all. I idealistically believed the government does not make laws that hurt its people; they are only supposed to make laws that protect, right? Therefore, I reasoned, abortion must be safe and good for women. It was not a baby yet—just tissue. Much of the recollection process is blissfully lost in a God-induced amnesia, but I do know I asked numerous times, and was always assured, it was still "just tissue." As a nurse, she was trained as a part of the medical profession. I assured myself, she should know. Well, it would certainly keep my life less problematic. I had to face it, her response worked for me.

I never really totally sold Gary on all the information, but he also concluded abortion would simply be easier. I had told him before our marriage I would love to give him a child someday, one that would be ours. But we had to be practical in these things. I rationalized to him that at thirty-nine years of age, the timing was all wrong and our lives were already full. I picked up the phone, dialing to set up the appointments.

The first appointment I made was for my counseling. Counseling? The word implies a conversation, talking out choices, and being led in the right direction. I arrived at the office and was walked into a sterile room with no windows or plants. There were precisely three objects in the room: a metal table and two chairs. After waiting for what seemed to be forever, a lady walked in with a file, sat down in the other chair, and began. It was so stark; I can still hear the entire interview verbatim....

"Your name is Kay?"

I affirmed her information.

"The father is aware we are talking about an abortion?"

Again, I quietly confirmed her words. After my response, she spun the file around, pushed it across the table to rest in front of me, and handed me a pen. I signed on the dotted line. That action condemned my daughter to death....

I blink a few times as the movie scenes relent momentarily. The outcome would be far different than what was explained to me by the doctor's nurse. Why had I been so blind? Selfishness had stood blocking my view of the harsh reality of my future. "Woe to those who are wise in their own eyes and clever in their own sight" (Isaiah 5:21). Sadly, I can now see the truth in Isaiah's words. My sight was impaired by my human judgment. God's sight is always perfect. Then, with barely a moment's breath, I was whisked back into the past....

After signing the papers, I was led to a little dressing room where I was to put on a surgical gown and wait. As I entered, I noticed again there were few accoutrements beyond the necessary ones in the room. Removing my clothing, I glanced at myself in the full-length mirror. I was surprised at what my reflection showed. My attention became fixated on the baby bulge I had just discovered there, slightly below my waist. Previously unnoticed in the mistaken belief I could not conceive, I placed my hand over the physical evidence of my baby. I found I was asking myself: *Are you doing the right thing? Is this really what you want?* Reassured with the list of reasons I had given Gary earlier, I knew to move ahead with the plan was the best thing.

Upon hearing my name called, I walked down the hall, and willingly crawled up onto the surgical table, like a goat being led to the slaughter. Once again, the medical personnel promised I could return to my customary routine in a few short days. Lying there in a prone position, I was inserted with what is called saline solution. I had been told it would not be painful, and discovering it to be factual, I began to relax as the procedure was efficiently completed. My next appointment would be a return visit in two days. At that time the removal of the "tissue" would be the last step. I noticed some minor discomfort, but in reality, the whole process was pretty much a breeze.

I grimace as the significance of all they had neglected to mention at the doctor's office and during my "counseling" session hits me. When it was many months too late, I would discover the omitted facts about the procedure. I squeeze my eyes shut as tight as I can and involuntarily flinch because I now understand: although I had only experienced some insignificant discomfort, my innocent baby suffered extreme pain as the liquid did its horrid job. Saline solution is composed of salt. This method of abortion literally burns the baby's flesh. At best guess, I was about four months pregnant. The pain I inflicted on my little girl would take years of healing for me to

overcome. But there was more to come as my
sins continued being laid out before me....

Returning for my second *trouble-free* appointment, Gary dropped me off at the door to the clinic. He was going to go visit a friend and would return in a couple of hours, about the time when I would be released. He claimed, "No need to waste time sitting in a waiting room. If something goes wrong, they can call me."

Draped in the hospital gown for the second time, I lay flat on the cold metal table. I had been given something that helped with the pain, but also aided in clouding the mind. When the man (I will never again call him a doctor. Doctors save lives—they do not take them!) completed the *extraction,* he made a terrible error in judgment. He had become so emotionally removed from the procedure, he simply tossed the extracted *tissue* into the metal garbage can by the head of my table. *Thud!*

Up until that moment in time, I had been completely tranquil.... *Thud!* I have regularly heard the sound replay itself many times over the subsequent years. That was no tissue! That sounded like flesh and bones! My mind raced back to the words: "It isn't a baby yet if we do this right away." When does it become a baby? At exactly what point is the miracle moment when it turns from tissue into a baby? My God! What had I done! I went from tranquil to hysterical in a split second. I began screaming uncontrollably, and the lady assisting curtly scolded me. "Stop! You are scaring the ladies in the other rooms! If you don't stop screaming, we are going to have to sedate you!" When I was unable to comply, I was given the threatened injection. By the time Gary took me home, I was in a drug induced state of peace. How could I have known the demons I would soon be facing?

There is no follow-up appointment after an abortion for any difficulties, whether they are physical, emotional, or spiritual that one might encounter. It is the only medical procedure of which I am aware, for which there is no medical review and checkup appointment. The philosophy is sad: The personnel have completed their jobs. The patient received the services for which she has paid. There is finality once the money has changed hands—

"Excuse me, would you like the pasta dish, the beef Stroganoff, or the fish?" The stewardess' words catch me completely off guard as I abruptly revisit reality.

"Beef Stroganoff, please," I reply, barely conscious of my answer. In the next moment, I return to the next frame of the movie, right where it had left off....

Lying in a fetal position and sobbing most of the time would eventually become my new habit. Each week would progress into the weekend. Then Monday would roll around all too soon, and I would have to go out and face the real world. Putting on a face of normality, while simultaneously constructing a wall of isolation around myself, I would head for the shop.

Oh, I longed to talk with someone—anyone, who would help me work through the traumatic effects of the events that had transpired. During that first weekend, Gary had been thoughtful, bringing me water, and encouraging me to eat. But the abortion itself was still too tender a subject for either of us to thrash out just yet. In addition, there was always the chance one of the girls would hear our secret if we talked about it at home.

Out of necessity, I began to be someone I was not. No one could ever know me—the real me, who I knew existed under the calm exterior. It was imperative that no one ever find out I murdered my own child. I truly earned, and deserved, an Academy Award for my all-inclusive performance. I fooled the entire world into believing there was nothing wrong. My Christian friends from church would surely be scandalized by even the suggestion of an abortion. No pastor could ever understand my predicament. And if I did work up the courage to discuss it with a pastor, his repulsion would be so great, his only possible reaction would be an addition to my already overactive guilty nature. The state I was in at the time, repulsion, horror, and guilt from anyone may have sent me into a downward spiral from which I would never have recovered. No one—not Gary, not the girls, not my friends, no one could be trusted. I never realized I was shutting out the very ones I needed, the ones who would have been willing to lead me to *The Answer*.

I established a whole new circle of friends. My new acquaintances were ones whom, if they did find out, would no doubt be more understanding of the circumstances than my previous companions would have been. Even so, I never allowed my new friends close enough to truly know me. No, I just built walls, built high walls to protect myself.

It would be years before I would allow anyone to draw near to me. Every time I allowed myself to think about letting someone in on my big secret, all I could think of was the rejection I deserved. Gary was unsympathetic because I was the one who made the decision. I was the one who willingly crawled up on the cold, metal table. I was the one who could have changed the circumstances. I was a murderer...who deserved rejection from everyone.

In outward appearances, I functioned as would any average person. I had to be *in order* to keep up the appearance of normality. However, inwardly, I was slowly being eaten alive with guilt and the indescribable remorse. They became my constant companions. My recent burgeoning self-esteem and confidence eroded under the weight of shame and self-hatred. The severe disconnect between God and I was a chasm, at best. No terminology of which I am aware can even begin to articulate the tremendous transformation my life took on after the abortion, and it was not for the better. I had believed I had personal problems before. Now I truly knew the meaning of personal problems. How could I ever have imagined how trivial my previous tribulations were in comparison to the echelon of trials I was experiencing now?

Nothing mattered! Day and night, I replayed the scene over and over in my head, the realization of the truth, the deep loss, the unbearable pain, and the finality of *The Thud*. For months afterwards, I would be awakened by screams in the night, sit straight up in bed, only to realize those horrifying shrieks were coming from me. It was too late for me...too late!

Every time I would awaken in fright, I would fall to my knees, praying. The Christian teachings of my early childhood would present themselves as an autonomic response to the terror. I would call out to a God, whom, I was sure, wanted no part of me—the murderer. I would plead with Him with a great hope He was listening:

> *If there is a way...any way...to wipe away this pain and guilt, please show me how. Who can I turn to? Who will understand? Who will have the answer—and not discard me? If You will grant me another miracle and give me another baby, I will be the best mommy in the world. I know I messed up Your last miracle, but I can be a good mother. I'd like the opportunity to prove it! Please, let me redeem myself. This time I'll do everything right....*

I would beg Him over and over, until in exhaustion, I would sleep.

With the morning light, returned my reality. There was no place to go! No one whom I could trust! I was now alone and getting precisely what I deserved. The answer to my troubles was so obvious, so simple, but in all the turmoil of shame, I could not or would not seek Him—*The Only Answer.*

Chapter Eight

Though I was slowly disintegrating, the relationship between Gary and I seemed to be doing better. Our grief had lost some of its sharpness, and the wounds had healed some. Although when we quarreled in anger, and in those times he wanted to win a disagreement, words of my *unspeakable secret* would always seem to appear. He knew I believed if the unfathomable secret ever reached the girls, I would lose absolutely everything. Because I had no doubt of that, those arguments would always end with him as the winner.

We became involved in several groups, and became quite the busy social couple. One of the groups in which we spent a great deal of time was based on Christian principles. They promoted the idea of God first, family second, business third. We began making friends who had their priorities straight. These people were secure in their relationships with God, in their marriages, as parents, and as business associates. The influence of our new friends made me wonder if maybe, just maybe, there was redemption available even for me. As Gary and I reconnected with organized religion, our drinking habits subsided. Gary's seductive ways were less pronounced because we were surrounded by happily married couples; there were no opportunities for that type of behavior. Gradually, our associations allowed me to take encouragement from them and permitted us to return to respectable living.

Then the unbelievable happened! God heard my pleadings! I was pregnant yet again. My redemption child was on the way! In silence, I claimed my forgiveness, a new beginning, and reiterated the promise I had made. *This time I'll be the best mommy in the world!*

In my joy I was lured into a false sense of forgiveness. I believed God was giving me my second chance. However, the lifestyle I had made for myself after the abortion remained unchanged. I should have realized if I had truly released myself from the guilt, if the knowledge of that forgiveness had really taken root in my heart, my life would have changed for the better. I would have acknowledged God's gift of healing. I would have been able to happily allow my friends to know the real me. My walls would have come down, and I would have enjoyed living a full life in God's presence.

Instead, fear and insecurity still ruled my life. I unrelentingly stayed aloof, reinforcing the tall barriers surrounding me and continued to leave everyone at an arm's length. I did not want, nor allow, anyone to do anything for me. The loathing and remorseful pattern continued.

There are many dangers in false forgiveness. It was bad enough to know I was in trouble, to know I had done something wrong and needed to fix the situation. The consequences of my actions were regularly laid out before me to see. However, when I began deceiving myself with the normal lifestyle, I was setting myself up for a colossal fall. I thought everything was returning to normal. I did not need to worry about anything anymore. I could behave as if the nurse's words were correct: "You do not have to ever think about it again." This deception would make the consequences far worse when the reality came crashing down. It would be quite some time before the collapse would happen, but it would take me by surprise when it did. There were signals I should have seen but did not.

I had a reoccurring dream from time to time which would reaffirm the kind of an aloof god to whom I thought it was I called out to....

The dream began with me standing on the end of a high diving board, on the precipice of the decisive jumping moment. The pool immediately below me contained no water. Instead, "Jesus" would be standing there with his arms open wide as he would urge me to jump. He coaxed me, assuring me he would surely catch me, after all, he loved me.

Eventually, his promises would lure me into a sense of safety and I would jump. Once the force of gravity had me well in its grasp, "Jesus" would drop his arms and begin to laugh at me as gravity propelled me towards the concrete below, screaming for mercy the whole way. He would laughingly tell me what a fool I was to trust him, yet again. I was so stupid, such a sucker; I believed him every single time! Did I not learn my lesson the last time he wooed me into jumping....

I would always awaken before I hit the bottom of the pool, but the deceiver would use this dream to reinforce my insecurity for years. I was on my own; even "Jesus" would not help me. **This dream would be one of Satan's weapons against me.** *The part of God's forgiveness I totally missed was this: God had forgiven me the first time I cried out to Him. It was me who had not yet forgiven myself. This would be the subject of many, many battles to come before God would win the war.*

Gary and the girls were excited about the new baby. Our friends were a little astounded that at our ages we would be so thrilled. After all, we were well beyond the normal age of expecting parents! This pregnancy was my most difficult one. Morning sickness was not just limited to the morning. I did not need a clock on the wall to tell the time because of its regularity. Every day it would first appear at seven o'clock in the morning. Next: eleven o'clock. Last occurrence: one o'clock in the afternoon.

The designers at the flower shop made up a song about my standing appointments in the bathroom. The vomiting started almost immediately after conception and continued throughout the next nine months, until just hours before my son was born. Even with the difficulties of my pregnancy, I continued with the facade of living a normal life. I appeared to have it all together. Yet hidden behind the tall walls, the real me was painfully alone and a complete spiritual mess.

Symptoms of my spiritual unrest would show themselves in my thinking patterns in times of stress. I hemorrhaged the first time while I was waiting on a customer at my shop. I began feeling strange; when I looked down, my feet were surrounded by a pool of blood. I managed to stay calm until the transaction was completed; then I immediately called my doctor. Panic was beginning to set in as I drove to the hastily arranged emergency appointment. It was far too early for my baby to be born. I still had about six months before he was supposed to arrive!

After the examination, I was told to go home and get some bed rest. The idle time in bed was spent thinking...not resting. Was God playing games with me? Was He playing a cruel game of cat and mouse? Did He give me this baby, only to take it away as punishment for my sins? I only increased the intensity of my promises to God. I would do better with this child than with my others. I would do anything to keep the baby safe. Please, Lord, let me be the mommy I know I can be!

Life continued. In our ever-present quest to make Full Bloom the best floral business in the area, Gary, Suzie, DeeDee, and I were miles from home at a Wedding Floral Conference. We had worked hard and submitted a plentiful array of fresh wedding floral items to be critiqued. There were bridal bouquets and bridesmaids' arrangements. We exhibited decorated candelabras, pew accents and alter garlands. Suzie and DeeDee served as our models, wearing striking gowns. Standing amidst the products over which we had slaved so hard the previous night, they showcased our merchandise to the judges. Our floral presentation was met with wide-spread approval. We would proudly display our plaques on the wall, giving our shop even more prestige.

As we were standing in line for a buffet breakfast the next morning, I began to bleed profusely. The car was quickly loaded by my family, as I lay in the backseat of the car with a pillow under the small of my back. With as much haste as possible, we rushed for the hospital near our home. The doctor's orders were the same as the last time, but more stringent: complete bed rest.

I was eagerly submissive. If this is what it would take to keep the promise I had staunchly given to be a *good mommy*, this time I would follow the orders to the letter and the spirit. I meant it with every fiber of my being: this time would be different. But would He allow it? Had He really given me this chance? Or did the game continue? I quieted the thoughts with a tentative assurance: I was pregnant and therefore forgiven.

⁂

After months of daily illness, two very frightening experiences, and what seemed like a millennium of worry, our handsome baby boy arrived. At his birth, he was very lethargic, which is a symptom of Meningitis, and they isolated him almost immediately. Was I still being punished? What if God took this child because I aborted the last one? It was so very hard to leave Kevin at the hospital when I was released. How was I supposed to be a *good mommy* if my child was not with me? Five days later, doggedly, I reminded myself: *don't blow this one when my redemption child comes home.*

We settled into a new pattern at home. The girls would argue over who would hold Kevin. Gary was more parental than I had ever seen him. We appeared to be a happy family once again. Perhaps I had been hasty in my thoughts towards my husband. Although he had been pretty thoughtless at times, occasionally he could be very sweet by bringing me flowers, or fixing breakfast and serving it to me in bed. He had an amazing sense of humor when he was not in one of his dark moods. I still loved him. Maybe I was partially to blame. I could be pretty infuriating myself. We were tied together more permanently now than ever before. We shared a child. Gary now had the child I had promised him before our marriage. Kevin would, without a doubt, bind us together like nothing else ever could.

Kevin was the joy of my life; I doted on him, perhaps more than was healthy. Ultimately, I would come to discover over-loving a child is one of the prevailing ways a woman responds to having a child after an aborted pregnancy.

I finally sold my shop; it was part of my promise to God. I had learned my lesson earlier. I had denied myself time with my family in order to make Full Bloom, well...bloom. I could not raise Kevin and dedicate the necessary hours to work. I was going to set aside the next seventeen years of my life and be a full-time housewife and mother, just like I had promised God. My new, beloved job was training, loving, and guiding my son, especially through the early, formative years.

Kevin played sports, which I had always loved anyway. Now I could live my life's dreams through him. Unlike my parents, who dropped me off at the door of the church, I attended services with him. I was lost, but Kevin was still innocent, deserving of a loving Savior.

I slipped further into my sense of false security. I could not imagine any events which could possibly be more devastating than those we had just survived. I truly believed I had finally dealt with the abortion, and my secret was safe. My marriage was healthier than I could ever remember. Suzie and DeeDee were getting old enough; I had to start thinking about them and their adult independence. Kevin would be raised in a stable, normal family environment. He would have a father and *good mommy*.

I would take him to church where he would be taught how God would want him to live. I would protect him from anything which could possibly hurt the perfect life I envisioned for him. I felt like I needed to—at any cost—to repay God for the blessing of my son. Realistically, I knew it would not be a life of rainbows and sunshine. We have to expect problems: stormy times are just part of life. God does not offer His children trouble-free living. Yet, waiting in the wings, was a more turbulent storm than any I could ever have predicted.

⊱ *Chapter Nine* ⊰

Gary had established himself as a teamster union truck driver and was high up on the seniority list with his company. His income was enough to allow me to hold the position for which I longed—housewife.

One day, about two years after I sold Full Bloom, Gary arrived at his terminal in Atlanta to deliver some materials he had picked up and was to take to headquarters. The company's gate was chained and padlocked. The sign on the gate announced the company had, without warning, claimed bankruptcy. Gary's secure, good paying job of twelve years, ended abruptly. The union hall found jobs for him here and there, but those infrequent job opportunities did not bring in enough income to meet our outgoing living expenses.

After a couple months of high financial stresses, Gary decided the answer to our woes would be to buy a truck of our own and become an independent trucking business. We searched around and found an employment prospect which gave us hopeful expectations. They alleged we would have steady work and be home almost every weekend. With these promises ringing in our ears, I dipped into my inheritance funds for the second time (the first time was to buy our dream house), and we purchased a truck. To our sad disillusionment, neither assurance proved to be true. Gary was gone for weeks at a time, often running out of work as well as money for his expenses.

Struggling to stay afloat, a chance to purchase parts and tires we knew were stolen was very tempting when offered. However, united, we resolved our truck was to stay legitimate. We would not permit illegal parts to be put on it. To ensure we did not accidentally and unknowingly fall into the trap, we paid retail prices for parts we knew were lawfully obtained for anything which needed replacement. With our truck business still struggling and in financial trouble, we both asked in dismay, "Why?" After all, we had remained morally and legally right. An acquaintance of ours who had purchased some of the illicit parts, and who even told us how to siphon diesel from other trucks into our own tanks, was making a good living. Why was God not doing the same thing for us? Were we not doing it His way? Somehow, He was suddenly my God, and He owed me. We had finally done something right, and yet His hand seemed to have pulled away from our business. Without looking back to the many transgressions we had knowingly and willingly committed in our lives, we asked ourselves, "Now where is He?"

On one particular run, it was imperative the truck make a deadline from Orlando to Atlanta. It was summer, and I had decided to accompany Gary while Kevin was out of school. I had studied to become a commercial driver, taken the Commercial Driver's License (CDL) test, and passed. Our primary hope was by having a second qualified driver in the family our truck might become more profitable. Although I hated driving the truck, it was a way to have family activities. Kevin and I could accompany Gary on long trips while Kevin was out of school. We could spend some quality family time together.

One night, I poured coffee down Gary, talked, sung, or did whatever was necessary to keep him awake and to arrive at the destination within the required timeline. With the task accomplished and time to spare, the company offered Gary a full-time position on a temporary basis. Within months, temporary had turned into a permanent position.

This was the opportunity for which we were waiting! We began to see more income than either of us had ever imagined. The jobs were demanding, and the deadlines were tight, but the benefits were well worth it. As we realized we were becoming prosperous again, Gary became convinced if one truck meant good money, more trucks meant even better money. I was not convinced we needed to expand. I had seen on the farm with Jeff how quickly a family business could deplete a household of their operating funds. Necessities, honest domestic necessities, would become unobtainable. The demands of the business–the family's income, and keeping it functioning, would take precedence over the home. But Gary was determined. Under protest, I utilized the balance of my inheritance funds, and we became the dubious co-owners of four trucks.

I worked as the dispatcher, and Gary drove one of the trucks. We were not a large trucking company, and could not offer the nonessential benefits, like insurance and permit advances that larger companies could. Therefore, finding qualified drivers could be a rather uncertain challenge.

In our desperation we found Agnes. She was more than qualified and really needed the work. In those times it was still hard for a woman driver to find a job; women's liberation had not yet arrived in the trucking industry. Gary and I discussed the situation of him driving with a woman. Despite my doubts, Gary repeatedly assured me he could never, ever cheat on me. Agnes was quite heavy set; her grooming lacked refinement, and she was not particularly hygienically inviting. In return of his promise, I assured him, I still trusted him even after some past minor infractions.

Although we did not have the perfect family life for which I had hoped, I believed Kevin was the leverage needed to ensure Gary would come home to me. It did not occur to me at the time Gary had left Liz and his three sons to marry me. At first, Gary's calls while on overnight trips came regularly, and I was confident we had made the right choice. Then slowly his calls lessened in frequency. When I called him, there was no reply. I became suspicious.

"Ma'am, your dinner? And what would you like to drink?"

"Coffee," I answered. Although the gentleman sitting next to me tries to chat while we eat, I do not feel like small talk. Playing with the food more than eating it, my mind kept retracing the story which was unfolding. As distressing as it was, I was

anxious to get back to the movie. "Stewardess, could you remove this tray, please?"

Gathering all my nerve, I confronted Gary about my uncertainties. He went ballistic with rage. Who was I to have accused him on an immoral issue? I did not have the right to ask! It was too late to have any doubts; she was already hired. I was trapping him in an uncomfortable employer-employee conflict by bringing my suspicions up now, and he did not appreciate it. If I was going to blame him, then he might as well enjoy the accusations.

From that moment forward, there were no phone calls and, even worse, absolutely no communication between us. When I would ask him questions, I was instantly rebuffed. There would be no discussion between us for anything. Soon he did not care if I heard calls from her on the occasions he was at home. He claimed those calls were all about business. He continued, "You had originally agreed to hire her. You can just deal with the fact we have to converse."

Unable to continue in the situation, I threatened to leave. Only then did he finally agree to see a counselor. We spent weeks with no progress; Gary unrelentingly denied any misconduct. He blamed all the accusations and evidence on my imagination. His actions were never in question; it was always my perception which needed to be analyzed.

Later, during a Sunday afternoon session, the counselor was persistently prodding at both of us. Disgruntled, Gary got out of his chair, stood at the window, and stared at the rain pouring down outside. Jamming his hands in his jeans pockets, he angrily blurted out, "Okay, I had sex with her! So what! It was just sex; it meant nothing." Then he turned, and his eyes glared at me. "But you accused me, and so I did it. I had never touched her until then. I have felt so dirty ever since. I can't fire her; she'll claim I raped her. I don't want to ever feel like this again. I've had it with secrets. She won't stay long, once I don't touch her again."

The counselor stopped the session at that point. "You need to go home and talk. You have to determine where your relationship will be going in the future."

We drove home without a word being uttered. Upon our arrival, I ran into the house to escape the rain. Sometime later Gary joined me where I was sitting in a stunned stupor on our living room couch. He began to excuse and apologize his behavior away. As he broke down in front of me, he flung these words at me, "If you simply hadn't challenged me, I never would have even considered Agnes."

Analyzing my own actions, it was not long before I convinced myself he might have been right. It was probably my shortcomings and insecurities which caused all the problems. Even through the heartache and fresh wounds, the love I felt for him was still there.

Agnes continued working with Gary for several more months. I never asked what went on during that time. I just did the best I could, living with it by not thinking about them...at all. Agnes's calls came intermittently. While on the phone with her, Gary's voice constantly sounded guarded and strained; he would frequently leave the room for privacy. I refused to face the reality of what might be going on, and just kept any reservations I had to myself; *Just let him be, and do not question his actions. It would be better for Kevin to have his Dad. What would I do if my doubts caused Gary to leave us?*

Resolutely, we began a new phase of life with counseling. We tried to embrace the Biblical values upon which it was based. Time after time in those sessions, Gary reminded me, "If you had kept your nose to yourself, I would never have slept with Agnes." The long forgotten insecurities from my relationship with Jeff resurfaced. I had again shown my worthlessness in marriage. Even though my heart was in tatters, time moved forward. *Who am I anyway? I am a nobody!*

Gary's affair with Agnes and the resulting guilt, in combination with our ominous financial conditions, plummeted him into a very severe depression. The doctors we consulted said not to leave him alone. He might be suicidal.

I had begun a babysitting service in our home some time before. We believed this would supplement our income while allowing me to stay home and be the good mommy I had promised to be to Kevin. Now it proved to be a convenient method of watching Gary. In his incapacitated state, he was unable to work. Naturally, this led to compounded problems with our budget deficit. As time continued, Gary resented my being his keeper. Our tempers clashed about the inevitable crumbling of our finances and how we were to handle money issues.

Heated discussions, clouded with bitterness of who was most important and who was the boss, would ensue but never be settled. Somehow life became routine again. Gary and I existed in the same house but as different beings. No interaction was better than fighting. I again hoped this was the last of the unexpected hurtles we would find. I was only fooling myself.

⚜ *Chapter Ten* ⚜

Each of the children acted out in their own ways and in their own times. Though at separate points in their lives, both Suzie and DeeDee would move in with their father for a few months. Their stays were only brief, and each of them would later decide to return to my home.

Oooh! Ouch! Reality hit in full force. Lord, I am mortified to comprehend how my past indiscretions negatively impacted the manner in which my two daughters would behave. Sadly, I have to concede on this point: I did not give them a good example, one which I wished for them to follow. Further yet, not only did I set this example here on earth, but as Your Prodigal Daughter, Father, I set the pattern in our spiritual lives as well: lured away from a good situation by the promise of something better, only to come running back to Your arms and home when the need arose. I am so sorry!

Suzie skipped twenty-three consecutive days of school before I received a letter. When I confronted her, she retreated to her room with shouts of how I was unfair. I honestly tried to talk with her, but she refused to utter a word. The next morning I discovered she had packed and vanished through the back sliding glass door, undetected. We spent days searching for her to no avail. Waiting for news of any kind was the worst. Was she all right? What kind of people was she with? What was she doing? Was she safe? Why was she not going to classes at school? It was a whole week full of fret and worry until she resurfaced. She had found a way to contact her father.

Jeff and Suzie had come to an agreement where Suzie would stay at his house. The arrangement was only temporary; within six months, Suzie would ask me if she could return to my home. She did come back, but with new rules which would apply to her schoolwork, dating, and keeping secrets. Gratefully and cheerfully, she agreed. Within the next year, Suzie would become a single mother. She continued living with Gary, DeeDee, Kevin, and I. She worked while I added my first grandson, Mark, to my babysitting business. He and Kevin would become great pals.

*

DeeDee met me at the front door one day after Mark joined our lives. DeeDee announced she had decided she wanted to go live with her father now. She said, "You play favorites with your children! You are too strict; I am incredibly unhappy. My new stepmother has a daughter near my age, and I like her. Besides all that, Dad understands me!" In anger, I went to the garage and grabbed some empty boxes.

I called Jeff on the phone and told him, "Come and get DeeDee! She wants to stay with you. I'm packing her clothes as we speak." Jeff arrived at my house to find DeeDee's clothes jammed helter-skelter into boxes, and DeeDee waiting on the front porch with her dog. Frantically, I assured myself, this was not of my doing. Jeff had obviously bribed her or something. Now DeeDee was gone, and I wondered what kind of fallout would arise because of this unwise move. But DeeDee had gotten what she wanted!

Several weeks later, Suzie came and advised me: DeeDee was bragging about the things she was getting away with, things of which Jeff was not aware. So I went to Jeff who told me I was simply pathetic and jealous. He did try to ease my mind, though, "Our daughter is fine." He snidely continued, "You had better get used to not having her live with you anymore. DeeDee will be permanently ours."

DeeDee stayed at Jeff's house for about seven months.

One Sunday afternoon, I heard a knock on our front door. Opening the door, I found DeeDee's stepmother. She announced, "DeeDee is out of control. If you want her back, you can have her! It's either that, or I'm taking her to Juvenile Hall, immediately. DeeDee has been slipping out her bedroom window and going to do her own thing—whatever it is she's doing. Her father refuses to punish her, probably because of his ego." She concluded with, "I don't want your daughter in my home any longer!"

I asked, "Where is Jeff?"

Sharply, she responded, "He's out of town; I want her gone when he gets home."

The second I said, "Yes, she can come home," DeeDee ran from where she had been standing, hiding in the bushes, unnoticed, and plunged into my arms. So DeeDee returned to us, more broken than when she left.

I suddenly remember the scripture about division: "Jesus knew their thoughts and said to them, 'A kingdom divided against itself will be ruined, and a house divided against itself will fall'" (Luke 11:17). I reminisce over what a house divided means. Had our lives at that time actually emulated its meaning? Divided? Now in retrospect, I realize we had been a house very divided.

Kevin loved his sports. I reveled in every football, basketball, baseball, and soccer game. My promise to be a *good mommy* involved my attendance at every event in his life, no matter how small an event it seemed. Gary did not take as active a role in Kevin's games. He believed if he attended one thing a week, his parenting obligations were concluded until the next week. People would regularly tell me I could never find fault with Kevin, and I was always taking his side. Gary would often say, "If you had to choose between Kevin and me, I'd lose." He would have; he simply was not aware of the oath I had taken before God when Kevin was born.

In the midst of many doubts, Gary and I continued to pretend our married life was normal, while an unspeakable cloud of distrust hovered over us. We had tremendous feelings of suspicion toward each other which would have to be overcome for our marriage to be fixed. We both seemed to work at it or at least that was the appearance. Days turned into months. Everyone in our house was unhappy; everyone walked carefully around the others. "Tread lightly" was our daily way of life.

I have heard somewhere, "It is a blessing we cannot see the future." The abuse at Jeff's hands, the adultery with Gary, the abortion of my child...these I now know to be the testing grounds at the beginning of my great sorrow. I marvel at God's wisdom. For if I had known what was still to come, I do not know if I would have had the courage to face the future....

❦ *Chapter Eleven* ❧

The tension in our unhappy home had been building, and I knew something had to give. Heavy despondency is a vast burden to carry. I was broken inside and on the outside. I was tired of having to appear to be fine. The nothingness I felt could not be eradicated by Gary, the girls, or friends. Even when we did family activities on the weekends with his boys, I still felt empty. I knew I had to find a way to end the feelings of worthlessness which plagued me every moment of every day.

Suddenly one day it all made sense; the answer was so clear! Why had it taken me so long to realize the solution was right in front of my eyes? Then I remembered: I was dumb.

I spent the next couple of days determinedly calling friends to reconnect with them. I had a habit of hiding cash in unlikely places around the house. When my task was complete, I wanted it all to be in one easy location. I cleaned house and did laundry. It took a couple days to get everything in place.

Once I had finished all of the preparations, I called Suzie. She had recently married and was living just a few blocks away. Since she was a housewife too, we frequently would drop our children off at each other's houses while we did short errands. My request was not suspicious. I took Kevin and another boy I was babysitting on that day over to Suzie's house. The scene will forever be etched in my memory, going back just one last time to give Kevin a hug and the bewildered look on his face. He knew something was not quite right, but did not understand.

Waving to them out of the car window as they stood in the yard, slowly and deliberately I drove away. "Good-bye, little one. I love you!" So much for the promise I made to be the best mommy in the world. I had only one way left to follow through on my pledge....

I had always been known for my fast driving. My grandson used to sing to me, "Go Gammy Go Gammy Go Gammy Go," as I flew down the road. It would just be classified as another tragic car accident. This accident promised to bring an end to the inexhaustible ache I was carrying inside. I thought I had looked everywhere to find a way to stop the pain. I did not realize I had not looked to the one place I should have: to God. But our relationship had been so distant, I could barely believe He would hear me, let alone answer. I should have understood He was right there in the car, next to me, crying at what His daughter was about to do.

My objective was to drive to the nearby freeway and accelerate into one of the concrete overpasses. Quick, clean, easy, and sure. I had not left a note behind. Who would care? I mentally checked my preparation list one last time as I pulled into the outside lane and began to pick up speed. I aimed for the mass of concrete which seemed to call to me. It promised the peace I had longed for and had not found anywhere else. The house was clean; I could not be accused of being a slob. The cash was no longer in the pocket of the third sweater from the end of my closet; I hid it in the cookie jar. I had called all my friends and family and said good-bye, without actually using those words. I had told my children "I love you" more frequently than normal; they would remember that when I was gone. I had done everything I could to make it easy for them when they realized I would not be coming home.

I had built up enough speed to ensure my death and the concrete pillar was now only a short distance ahead. The life insurance money would help alleviate the financial problems in the home. My death would be the end of the marital problems. My son would no longer have to endure the fighting and tension. This was, indeed, the perfect answer—the right answer.

Here I go.... I flinched as I aimed the car and could not bring myself to complete the task. I drove to the next exit only to turn around and go back time and time again. *If I could only do this,* I told myself, *everyone would win.* Yet, I was such a loser I could not even rid my family of a blight—me. No one else needed to be hurt; I just needed to eliminate the source of the problem—me! I was such a miserable excuse for a human being, always doing or saying the wrong thing at the wrong time.

Living was a horrible mistake—a terrible way to exist. What kind of a god would create something like me? Did he do it to entertain himself, get his kicks out of watching someone like me struggle? I did not realize He had just saved me! If I had ended my life right then, His plans for my future would not have been carried out. I had no idea, could never have imagined, what He had planned for me, lying ahead in my future.

Heading home from yet another failure, I made myself a vow I would just be me, bumbling along day after day. I would try to stop thinking about me and my needs. I would do my best to please others. Then at least those people would see something of worth in me. Even though I had not managed to hit the concrete, my dreams and aspirations for my life died out there on that freeway as surely as if I had completed my goal. Maybe I could find some purpose in life if I just fulfilled what everyone else expected of me. Then they might at least act as if they cared.

I had spoken of my despair a few times, but my words had been met with either ridicule or a scoff. It was my way of saying "help me," but the cry fell on deaf human ears. The one I should have been crying out to was the Lord. But in my agony, I could not believe He would care.

I recall admiring a beautiful yellow diamond ring in a jewelry store window and thinking, *God just made such beauty to show me what I do not deserve. He only put it there to tantalize me.* I still had not really internalized the love God has for His children. I still had some more lessons to learn before I could understand the depth of His caring.

<hr />

One of the ways in which I fulfilled the needs of others, but not for myself, was to purchase clothes for the family. I went several years without one new garment. Since no one cared about me, they were not looking at my wardrobe. I can recall my bra was so worn, it was held together by five safety pins. Suzie was finally able to coax me into going to a thrift store to see about some new-to-me clothes. When I finally did join her on a shopping spree, I came home with twenty-five dollars' worth of clothing and a huge burden of guilt. Why had I wasted so much on myself? I smile as I think about my current shopping habits. My third husband, Doug, shudders when I grab the checkbook and head for a bargain store. What a change from the mindset of guilt and uselessness, from where I was back then. God brought back a short memory to emphasize the difference in another way as well...

I had told a friend of mine one day as we took a walk, I have not cried in five years. I was bragging about it. "I bet you cannot make me cry. You can try your hardest, but won't succeed." With all of the pain which had peppered my life, most of it self-inflicted, I had trained my mind to protect myself from any emotions. I would simply shut down.

I realize the day would come, however, when I would have to acknowledge I never really allowed God to be a part of my daily life. This was the God from whom I ran, but He had always been waiting patiently on the outer edges of my consciousness.

My life was like a puzzle God was putting together. Jigsaw puzzles have outer boundaries which define the shapes they will eventually take. It seems the natural place to begin when putting a picture puzzle together. Once those boundaries are established, the inside of the puzzle is much easier to put together. God revealed, even while I was running and hiding, He was putting this outer edge of my life together. Then, as I began to acknowledge Him and follow His path, slowly, He began to reveal some of His bigger plans for my life. He began putting some of those interior pieces in place. Once we stay within His parameters and guidelines, He begins transforming us into His likeness. But there were countless lessons left to learn before I would be able to let Him in enough, He would be able to show me more of the picture it contained.

Our finances decayed, and the income we earned shrunk in comparison to our expenses. We never had the full fleet of trucks in running condition at the same time. Sometimes a truck needed repairs. Sometimes one of the trucks was down for routine maintenance. Sometimes one of the drivers would refuse to do as directed. Sometimes there were no deliveries to be made.

Unfortunately, a few of the companies, for whom we inadvertently drove, were less than honorable. They would change their names and phone numbers, leaving us no method to locate them. Therefore, we would not receive payment for services rendered; only exacerbating the problem of our dwindling operating funds, despite the lack of income, wages, fuel bills, and road taxes all came due, regardless of our situation.

My babysitting business and odd jobs I found had not significantly eased the financial pressures. Doing what we could was not enough; our expenses far outweighed our combined income. Our credit cards were used until we were at the maximum credit amount, and something had to change.

A second mortgage was taken out on my dream house. It was still as beautiful as when I had used my (now non-existent) inheritance funds for the first time to make the down payment. Because of the large deposit, our monthly mortgage payments were quite reasonable. Now with the second mortgage on the house, the monthly expense exceeded our comfort limit. However, Gary assured me, it would be only temporary.

Within months, the balances of all our credit opportunities were again at their limits. It became painfully apparent—nothing was working. We placed my dream house on the market and purchased a smaller, but nice, home only a few miles away.

If I knew then what I know now, this move would never have taken place. It was the beginning of the ultimate catastrophe in the lives of Kevin and me. It would not be long before my family was in tatters, and I would be on my knees, crippled by the weight of the heartbreak. Nonetheless, it would also be the beginning of my real healing.

God, even now, in retrospect, I'm still thinking my way. If it had not been for this move, Your plan for my service to You would have never come to be....

❧ *Chapter Twelve* ❧

The new house, even with far lower payments, became delinquent; history was repeating itself. As a result, I realized I would have to find a job, and find one quickly. Kevin was now a teenager. Although my vow to God to be near Kevin whenever he needed me was important, our immediate needs like food and clothing were more pressing.

Every day we were receiving delinquency notes of one kind or another. We were behind on our credit card payments; the finance company was threatening repossession of three of our trucks. No matter how I stretched our meager income, we were continually slipping further into debt. I accepted a position at a local bank in their customer service credit card department. Even with the new income, it became clear. Though we hoped to avoid it, we would inevitably have to file bankruptcy. We were left with no trucking fleet, no rainy day inheritance funds—no dream home.

After several months of unemployment, Gary got a job at a local electronics department store for a minimal salary, plus a commission on any computer he sold. With his work experience for more than two decades in truck driving, Gary's knowledge base about computers was non-existent, and he was unable to contribute enough for our house payment, much less the utilities or car payments. Our finances plummeted yet again.

I pleaded with Gary, "Get a second job, or *please* go back to driving a truck." But he was unyielding. Gary swore to me he would never drive a truck again. He would never put himself in the position of driving with a woman or being away from Kevin and me overnight. I told him it did not have to be a permanent job, just long enough to help with the bills. He still refused to drive commercially to increase our financial standing. Stubbornly, he declared he was already doing everything he could to get us back on our feet. Why did I always compel him to do more? Do more!

About three months into my new job, the bank started a conversion on their computer systems, resulting in many positions becoming overwhelmed with a higher workload. It was a real blessing when my position was given unlimited overtime. Compared to our debts, however, even with the increase in funds, there would not be enough money to meet the backlog of late payments. So I took on three other jobs as well. I simply was not going to allow this house to slip away too.

My weekly schedule quickly became hectic. I would work at the bank on weekdays from five o'clock in the morning to six o'clock at night. All day Saturday, as well, was spent working at the bank. On Wednesdays and Thursdays, I would drive directly from the bank to a gift store in the local mall where I would work as a sales clerk until nine o'clock. Sundays consisted of a twelve hour shift standing on my feet doing manual labor on the production belt for a computer manufacturer. Lunch hours were not leisurely; I helped a friend clean houses for which she paid me in cash.

Gary would not, or possibly could not, do more to help the again growing deficit we faced. Soon I grew bitter, and he grew even more complacent. I was too exhausted working almost eighty hours a week to do more than just be an occasional presence in our home. My consolation was the mortgage was current, and the bills were being met. That had to be worth something.

Time passed; distrust grew. Gary and I communicated only in acidic sarcasm designed to injure. The distance between us grew larger. With all the regrets in our relationship, the adultery, the trucking disaster, spending my inheritance, losing my dream home, the resentment of four jobs versus one, I found myself unable to put forth the effort needed to repair the relationship with Gary again. He toppled off the white horse; he was no longer my knight in shining armor, my hero. We developed a total disregard for each other.

Kevin, now fifteen, stayed in his room and would turn up the music to drown out the discord in the house. He occasionally had friends over, but more often, he went to their houses to escape his own home. This was disturbingly similar to what I had experienced once before; it was exactly how the girls had behaved. The only common denominator I could find in my exhausted state was me! I had come full circle in my life and it was starting all over again.

There was also another parallel unfolding in the household. Ever so slowly, I became aware of an unspecified threat, matching one from years before. His language and actions appeared to be identical. I recognized Gary's heart was missing from our marriage. I became suspicious all over again as all the old symptoms began to emerge. Gary was careful, always guarded in his conversations with me. He was actively avoiding family activities. There were strange, lengthy, seemingly pointless errands which had to be done by him. He was constantly belittling me and Kevin. I recognized the anguish from before, and realized he was validating his feelings and actions for another woman. I could not deal with another affair. I simply could not add that encumbrance to my already plagued life.

I did not want my marriage to end. I was not currently capable of seeing Gary as the loving husband I once desired, but I wanted to! I knew it was beyond our limited capabilities to repair the damage we had both inflicted on our union, but I was willing to try many things to avoid a second divorce. I had seen what happened to Suzie and DeeDee when Jeff and I divorced. Trying to avoid those consequences in Kevin's life, I urged Gary to attend counseling again. Halfheartedly, he agreed.

We had sometime earlier begun regularly attending a church, believing we were headed on the right course. Jesus was always calling to me—His precious daughter, trying to get me to come back into His house. This fact is revealed in how many times we *got on the right road* by attending church. When we were regularly attending services, Gary was a model citizen. He would not embarrass me in front of our church friends. Then suddenly, he sullied my safe haven....

One very rainy Sunday night, Gary dropped me off under the covered entrance to our church, and drove off; I believed, to park the car. I rejoiced in the fact he had been so thoughtful. He wanted me to stay dry. Church began a few minutes later; he did not appear. When the service was over, Gary was still missing. I was forced to ask one of Kevin's friends to drive me home. Walking through the front door when I arrived, I found Gary laid back in his recliner, a cup of coffee in his hand, watching a movie. He belligerently explained, "I never said I was going to attend the service."

Embarrassed and humiliated, I went to the bedroom, where I could display, in private, my rage and disillusionment. Kevin arrived home a little later, and had clearly heard the news. My son spouted a few choice, very special words at his egotistical father, before he tapped on my door. My spirit withered even further as Kevin tried his best to comfort me; I endeavored to make light of the whole incident. This was not the environment or life I had so vigilantly tried to design for him.

Later, Gary angrily approached the bedroom door, simply to announce, "Two against one, so what else is new?" Turning briskly, he clumped back down the hall to spend the night sleeping on the couch.

We asked for help from the pastor. With our overburdened finances, we could not afford to pay a counselor. The pastor would not charge us for his time but had only one request: to be truthful at all times, no matter what the personal cost. "Don't waste my time with lies. If you can do that, I can help you." We spent scores of nights in his office after work. Time and again, Gary denied any affair. He claimed my overblown imagination was working overtime; it was me which was the problem.

"If you only put as much time into our marriage as you do into trying to catch me in a fantasy affair, we would be happy," would be his frequent challenge to me.

Before our marriage Gary assured me he could never cheat on me. Nonetheless he already had. Recalling how shoddily he felt the last time, I mistakenly, and hopefully, thought he could never do it again. His promises, repeatedly conveyed since the affair with Agnes, served as reassurance to what I wanted to believe. His current, constant denials in counseling made me question my own self. The long ago doubts were whispering in my ear. I started to think it was almost certainly my inadequacies which distorted reality into something distasteful. If I indeed was wrong, and there was no adultery going on, I would have to apologize. Could we actually repair the damage? Would it be possible to overcome the distrust? It would feel good to be secure in my marriage again. If not, how would I survive another divorce? What if my suspicions were confirmed? If he was again having an affair, could we work through it one more time? Or was our holy union to be like Humpty Dumpty and never be put together again?

I mused about the possibility of this payback for the affair I had so voluntarily participated in with Gary years earlier. The suggestion of being betrayed all over again made me reflect on the agony I had brought on Liz and even Jeff. Why had I been so willing to believe if Gary had an affair with me when he was married to Liz, his eye would not wander again? Jeff had done a lot of callous things to me, yet he in no way deserved what I had done to him.

Why do we call it an "affair?" Funny nobody calls it what the Bible does anymore: "adultery." Perchance the reason is because "affair" is more palatable to the ear.

Then there was my innocent child. I had effortlessly justified an "abortion." Had I called it by its real name, "murder," justification would not have been so easy. If we read the Bible more, and listened to colloquial language less, our lives would be far less complicated.

When divorced, both partners play a competitive sport called the "blame game." This is undoubtedly one of the many reasons God hates divorce. It splits not only finances and emotions, but loyalties as well.

The movie was showing me, once again, the mess I had made of my life by not heeding Biblical advice. Sadly, the damage had been done to all our family members years before, mostly thanks to me.

I wryly grin as I recite Jeremiah 29:11 to myself: "For I know the plans I have for you...plans to prosper you and not to harm you, plans to give you hope and a future."

God was not participating in any payback scheme. Instead, the plans God had for me were certainly more than I could have ever imagined myself. Only now can I appreciate all the preparation God had to do on me to make me realize I did have a place in His plans....

The counseling sessions seemed to follow the same repetitious patterns as the previous ones. Gary accused me of being crazy. I had embellished the truth on the number of hang up calls, his incessant need to leave at specific times—for impractical reasons—only to return far later than the stated errand required. He did reply when I said, "I love you." His reply would be, "Yes, I know" or "Me, too." So what! He never echoed the words back to me and never uttered the word "love" to me anymore. Gary said I was just looking for any reason to find fault with him, and I was doing a first-rate job of it.

The situation finally eroded when Gary became adamant. He was unwavering in his determination to move into the spare bedroom—for a little while. The previous night, I made a request of him to turn down the volume of the TV some so I could sleep. It gave him the excuse he needed. It did not take a genius to see what was happening; in fact, I was a veteran at it.

> *Do not be deceived, God is not mocked. A man*
> *reaps what he sows.*
>
> > *Galatians 6:7*

Maybe the verse should have read "A *woman* reaps what she sows." Was I about to reap again what I had sown years earlier? Would I now taste again the bitterness of what I had sown to Jeff, in my frenzy to find a new and happier life? I fell back into the old pattern: being a nothing, I deserved and should expect—nothing.

Chapter Thirteen

The smaller house we purchased was in a friendly neighborhood, and we had made some great friends. Across the street one household became like family. We would regularly share meals together, sit and reminisce about our day's events, and share our hopes for the future.

Another family of friends was immediately next door. Ellen was a single mother of two teens. She recently had to have a surgical procedure, a hysterectomy, so Gary and I helped with the kids, meals, and housework. It felt good to be able to serve someone else. After a few weeks, I realized there was more to *their* relationship than merely neighbors.

My suspicions were confirmed one Saturday night. A couple of friends dropped by unexpectedly and Gary offered to make coffee. I thought he went to the kitchen to begin the coffee percolating and then would return to visit with our guests. Instead, for what seemed like an interminable lifetime, I was the sole hostess. I became uncomfortable, excused myself for a moment, and peeked into the kitchen. He was chatting with someone on the phone. The moment he saw me, he dropped the phone, and began busying himself getting cups. I smiled and disregarded it for the moment, but he would have to provide some answers when we were alone.

At long last our friends left, and my time came to confront Gary about his little phone call. He fervently and angrily denied even being on the phone. He belligerently stated I was just over dramatizing again and should forget it. With a tenuous and unprecedented courage, I walked across the room, picked up the phone, and hit redial. Ring...ring..."Hello, honey!" came the familiar voice on the other end.

I hung up and glared at Gary straight in the eye. "That was Ellen. What were you doing calling her? And why is she calling you 'honey?'" He, again, denied ever dialing her. Raising my voice in complete anger, I said, "Well, someone dialed it. Somehow her phone number got on our kitchen phone as the last number called. It wasn't me!"

With an almost evil, insolent smile, Gary answered my implied accusation. "Well, it was probably Angel." He turned, went out the door, and drove away. Yes, I believed I was useless, but even I was not so dumb as to believe our dog was capable of making a phone call and having an intimate conversation with our neighbor! Upon arriving home from work every subsequent night, my first action would be to hit the redial button. Each time I would find myself listening to the latest weather forecast for our area. Gary had been trapped once but never again.

I jump as the lady on my right startles me by asking to get access to the isle. I intentionally act preoccupied so as not to have to idly converse with the gentleman who wanted to chat earlier. Shortly, the lady returns, and reluctantly I allow the cinema to restart. This was a part of my life about which I was not thrilled to revisit....

Incidents from the proceeding weeks began to replay again in my mind in great detail. The times I had called Gary and he was "out in the yard and didn't hear the phone." The times Ellen had dropped by just to say hello. The Easter concert at church: Since I was in the choir and had to arrive early, Gary offered to pick Ellen up and take her home. That Easter afternoon, we had snacks of homemade shortcake and strawberries. The two of them had a conversation all by themselves and were oblivious to my presence in the room. Ellen was now sporting lipstick and mascara; she had also updated her hair style. There were suspicious interactions and eye contact between the two of them. Call it naiveté or denial, I had previously overlooked all of these indications.

The mountain of evidence continued to grow. Gary had been doing crafts for several years. When our finances became desperate, he used this trade to supplement our income, and we had several prominent gift shops in resort towns which sold our products. I began remembering how many times I would go out where Gary was working, only to find Ellen just visiting.

Gary had increased the number of hours he spent in the garage shop, but his production had decreased by a significant factor. When I challenged him about the discrepancy, he glared vehemently at me, "Nothing I ever do for you is good enough, is it? I just can't please you," and marched into his bedroom slamming the door. Then I heard a second bang! The 4x4 was in place. He was again utilizing the barricade he had erected to ensure I could not follow him into his room. I still battled with the conviction: we can make this work.

Several days later, I had a dental appointment and did not leave for work at my usual time. It was ten o'clock when I drove by Ellen's house. One of her garage doors was open, revealing it to be crammed with craft items identical to the ones Gary sold. I wanted to go back for the camera to substantiate my claim, but if I did, I would be late for my appointment. It appeared she was storing some of his work. But was she selling our crafts? Where was the money going?

The answer came later that week when I retrieved the daily mail. Amid the envelopes was a statement from an unfamiliar bank. The names jumped off the envelope at me, and I had confirmation something nefarious was happening. The envelope displayed Gary's full name right beside Ellen's name with her address as the delivery destination.

My hands trembled as I ripped the envelope open. They were selling his crafts, had opened a joint savings account, and now had a balance of over two hundred dollars! Confronting Gary that evening, he rationally explained he had done something I had always encouraged him to do: opened a business account. I pointed out it had Ellen's name and address on it. He tried to tell me the address was put in the system incorrectly, but could not explain why her name appeared next to his name. He just smirked when he walked away. Going to his new bedroom, he placed the board in front of the door.

With my heart broken and filled with disillusionment, I persistently clung to the belief our marriage could still survive. Despite all the lame excuses and obvious lies, I just could not bring myself to face the inevitable. Denial is a very strong emotion, and when invoked, can excuse, justify, or explain away even the most compelling of evidence.

⁂

I was standing in the backyard one dark night. Ellen's two-story house was right next door to our ranch style one. I noticed her standing in the upstairs window with the light on behind her. She was standing there blowing kisses to someone in our front yard, evidently Gary, and mouthing, "I love you." I wanted to strangle them both! It took a few days before I finally accepted reality. I acknowledged the coming divorce, at last.

When I did, I employed rather unorthodox methods to assure I knew what was happening and was prepared for what might lie ahead. I purchased a recorder, the type which you place between the phone and the wall. An extended tape would record hours of calls for me, incoming and outgoing, and would shut off after each conversation.

Kevin's room was a typical teen's disaster; so I placed the recorder under his bed: the perfect, undiscoverable spot. My heart sank when I listened to the first recordings and recognized the voice on the other end of the line: Ellen. Validation of my suspicions was more painful than words can convey. However, within a day or two, I was aware of all the plans Ellen and Gary were making.

As I monitored the tapes daily, it boggled my mind how he would vilify me. He nitpicked everything about me and complained incessantly to her: "She does not appreciate anything I do. She has stopped doing my laundry. She won't fix my lunches, or prepare dinner for me. The house is a disaster; it looks like a cyclone hit it." In actuality, I had been purposely preparing his favorite foods. I was doing his laundry, and the house was cleaned regularly, even with my frantic schedule.

Where did all these lies come from? He was being deceitful to Ellen! It was a defining moment; I realized how hard Liz must have tried to defend her family when Gary had, very probably, lied to me about Liz. I prayed in vain for a miracle, but history was repeating itself.

Holding down four jobs, my time at home was limited. When I was home, I was exhausted. Gary, on the other hand, with only one job outside the home, had virtually unlimited time for his latest fascination—Ellen. It quickly became obvious Ellen was more than just a simple infatuation. Tenacious as I was, discouragement set in. In their phone calls, they discussed when Gary should leave, what to do about Kevin, and how to handle me when the time came.

On one notable occasion, they discussed how nice it would be if they could simply *eliminate* me from the picture altogether. They would have my son, our home, and my life insurance. What a great guarantee for the beginning of their promising new life together!

I was living a nightmare I had once lived before, only this time I was on the losing end of the battle; I was the one to be left behind. Eventually, I was unable to physically or emotionally handle the monitoring and a couple of my good friends took over. They would pass on needed information and protect me from the vilification.

Kevin was to be spared as much, and as long, as possible. That was my topmost priority. The looming divorce would be hard enough for him. Certainly, I could not shield him from all the pain, but I would protect him from as much of the nastiness as was feasible. I might be dumb, gullible, and unswervingly loyal, but I vowed I would not be taken advantage of or caught off guard.

I would be ready for their big surprise. I made a list of things for which I should prepare. First, I moved the guns to a friend's house, and felt safer. I resolved if Gary asked where they had gone, I would play dumb—certainly an easy and natural role for me to play. I had ignored all the indications as my world eroded despite everything I attempted to stop it.

Once again, the illusion I had for my life had been fractured. Then, I attempted to obtain a restraining order to protect myself. I was frustrated by the court system, which said there had been no physical abuse; verbal threats were not enough of an imminent danger to grant the restraining order.

The following Sunday after church, while Gary sat in his recliner in the family room watching football, I trimmed the shrubs which edged the fence around our backyard. Behind one particular bush something caught my eye; it was fresh wood. Closer examination disclosed a gate had been recently built between Ellen's backyard and our own. There was no latch. It was being held shut with a heavy flower pot, on her side of the fence to ensure its closure. My heart felt like it sunk down into my shoes. I ran, sobbing to the bedroom which had been mine alone for some time.

Gary simply watched as I ran by him; he did not understand, or care, what happened to upset me. I called the pastor from my room and through the tears, explained what I had just discovered. He assured me as best he could; we would have to deal with many such issues in time. I faced the undeniable certainty; my marriage with Gary was coming to a swift and unhappy ending.

One of the recordings revealed Ellen prodding Gary about money. She insinuated by working all the jobs I did, I probably had a secret bank account somewhere. She suggested an amount of eighty thousand dollars tucked away securely out of his reach. I laughed at her remark; it was beyond obscene. How did she come up with that amount? And if I had so much money hidden, why did I continue to work day and night to pay the bills? I could sure use the money at this point.

On another day, Ellen had told Gary when he left, he was to take all financial help with him. "Because if you help her, then you might as well just stay where you are."

With this revelation, I sat down and planned a workable budget for Kevin and me. I also began hunting for an apartment which Kevin and I could share. It needed to be one which allowed Kevin his space, but small enough I could afford to pay the rent on my income alone. I knew we had a short time to find something suitable, but vowed it would be accomplished before I was out of funds.

I promised myself I would not be caught off guard again. So I began getting ready for what seemed to be imminent. I might be a glutton for punishment, but I would be prepared.

The next thing I did to prepare was to borrow a video camera and established custody of all the house furnishings and his tools. I had to have proof. If he denied removing items from the house, or the value of his power tools, I would be left destitute. I felt I required some insurance, just in case. In a moment of vindictiveness, I took a picture of the newly acquired gate hidden behind the shrubs in the backyard too. Just simply because I could!

I called a friend—as close of friends as I allowed into my life; she happened to be a realtor. She had sold the flower shop and my dream home for me. Through several business interactions, I realized she was a good, honest person who truly desired to help those with whom she worked. I shared with her the situation in which I found myself.

The next afternoon she came and assessed the house and gave me a sale value. She took into account the half completed paneling on the family room wall, as well as the broken garbage disposal. With everything I showed her, it quickly became apparent Gary had already begun distancing himself from Kevin and me. His body was still present in our house, but his heart had already packed up and moved.

DeeDee, who was married and living in another state at this time, sent me a card to cheer me up; it had a bookmark enclosed. Along with a serene picture, there was this scripture: "Do not fear, for I am with you; Do not anxiously look about you, for I am your God. I will strengthen you; surely, I will help you. I will uphold you with My right hand" (Isaiah 41:10 NAS). After years of ignoring God, this Bible passage caught my attention. I claimed the verse, with a certainty He was going to fix my marriage somehow. When I read *"anxiously* look around you," it registered. This verse was especially for me! I had spent hours, days in fact, doing just that. I was *anxiously* watching Gary. I was *anxiously* watching Ellen. I was *anxiously* watching the mail, the woodcrafts, and the tools. God had actually shown me He was aware of what I was doing and, even after all I had done, was willing to help me. The timing was perfect, as is always God's timing. Her bookmark arrived just days before Gary would physically leave.

Gary told Ellen, "I think she has found someone too. She is smiling and walking around the house in a daydream," that day on the recording. I grinned, just a little. Upon hearing those words, it would be Gary who had the big surprise coming—not me! God was going to fix our marriage, and his relationship with Ellen would be terminated.

At times, we humans believe we have God all figured out. We know exactly how He is going to help us or answer our pleas. I smile as I think about how assured I was, for I knew God's tactics. Many years, after my willful sinning, which I called independence, I thought I knew what He was going to do to help me. Looking back, I realize this belief that God was working with me was the first of many cracks He would make in the walls I had built after the abortion. I was letting go of the saying "If it is to be, it is up to me." God was with me! He would help me and give me strength. He would, indeed, be my strength and right hand, but, as I was about to ascertain, it would not be in the way I had envisioned....

The tapes by no means revealed a date for his exodus, but I knew it was close—very close. Yet, I also knew God had given me a promise. He had said He would help me. How else could He do it, if He was not going to save my marriage? After all, I did not want another divorce. My heart cried out to God, *Please let me remain married.*

It was a Thursday, but something was different; I had sensed it all day. I found myself incapable of defining exactly what *it* was which had me restless. The day had begun like any other: leaving for work, the customary chit-chat during my lunch break, no unusual drama.

As I drove home and rounded the corner on our block, the house appeared to be the same. I especially remember feeling the warm, summer sun kiss my face, as I stepped from the car and walked toward the house. Even as I walked up the sidewalk, the feeling of malcontent and discomfort grew stronger. I entered the code to disable the house alarm and went to the kitchen, where a slow-cooker of my homemade stew had been simmering slowly since early morning. The aroma filled the rooms with a welcoming scent of home and family.

Then as my eyes fell on the clean kitchen counter, I saw them: a garage door opener and a set of house keys lay neatly side-by-side. Dazed, I dropped my purse on the dining room table. My apprehension grew as I turned and staggered to the garage.

Opening the connecting door, my worst fears were confirmed: His tools and all of his woodworking equipment were gone. Still unable to grasp the complete meaning of the missing items, I moved down the short hall filled with family pictures to the bedroom I still thought of as ours. Only later would I realize the picture frames of his family were empty. The closet door stood wide open; the place where his clothes had previously dangled, with a few exceptions of scattered items which hung in disarray, it was bare. Even as I wiped away the tears now tumbling down my cheeks, I smiled helplessly.... His Bible was gone too. *Well*, I thought to myself, *he sure needs that!*

It had happened sooner than I expected, but then, would I have ever truly been ready for this? Even though I had finally seen the signs, I did not want to be the one to leave the marriage. I had been the instigator of the divorce with Jeff. I had been the one who was Biblically wrong in that disaster. I did not want to take the responsibility on myself of being the one to end this relationship. So I had stayed. But this time, Gary had moved out.

Whether the tears were from sadness, or from relief the nightmare had finally ended, I was never sure. I dropped onto the bed we had once shared. I allowed myself the luxury of releasing all the pent up frustration and pain I had carried for months. I cried until I was sure there were no more tears; my eyes were very swollen, bloodshot, and hot. I ranted: How could he throw all our dreams away? How could he leave the plans for our future shattered by his betrayal? Then I realized, although we had existed in the same house these past few months, I had already been living alone. Now it was official...this marriage was over.

Kevin would be home soon. This painful news would not be able to be hidden from him after he walked through the door. I wanted to lessen the impact of the news that his father was having an affair; although I eventually found out he had been aware of it before me. I put cold compresses on my eyes, ran my comb through my hair, and added a touch of lipstick. I wanted to be physically primed, as I prepared to share the distressing emotional news with him.

I remember turning on the television. As the weather analyst predicted, the next day would be another beautiful summer day. I thought, *my life is virtually over and the rest of the world does not know...or care.* My musings were interrupted when I heard the screen door slam. My handsome son breezed in and dropped his homework on the couch. The moment his eyes met mine, his face turned white.

"Dad's gone, isn't he?" I nodded my head in simple response to his question. He walked over to me, wrapped his arms around me, drew me as close as he could, and said, "That's okay, Mom. I'll be the man of the house, and we'll be fine."

"No!" I broke down and sobbed in his arms. "That's not what I want for you! I want you to be a typical teenage boy, enjoying your senior year in high school."

We changed the code on our house alarm; Kevin and I had our sanctuary where Gary and Ellen could no longer intrude. Then we sat down and ate the homemade stew whose aroma warmly met me only a scant time ago, just the two of us. This would rapidly become our typical family dinner—just Kevin and me. Purposefully and deliberately, neither Kevin nor I glanced at the head of the table, at the place which now sat conspicuously vacant.

We each struggled with the emptiness in our own way, both wanting to support the other, but it was all we could do to hold ourselves together. My heart ached for this young man who stood before me. Clearing the table, I could tell he worked hard to disguise his pain, while trying to ease mine.

Who would be his example of a Christian father and husband? I reassured myself that God understood the deep pain Kevin was experiencing. Jesus, God's own Son, was rejected too. God could, and would, be an example for my son. He had already promised He would be in His Word: "A father to the fatherless, a defender of the widows, is God in His holy dwelling" (Psalms 68:5).

I alerted the pastor, who had been our counselor, of Gary's departure and what Kevin and I had done. The pastor advised I had one more thing which needed to be done. "Call Gary's sons. Share with them Suzie and DeeDee's experiences with Gary. I want you to specifically warn them about when Gary visited their rooms when they were still young."

I argued, "Their father has just left me. The boys are going to think I am being vindictive. They will not listen to me!"

"It is your duty to warn them," he countered. "They are now fathers of young girls. What they choose to do with the information is not your responsibility." After prayer, I called Liz.

Liz, whose husband I had literally stolen; Liz, who had been generous to me in every way through all those years; Liz, whose grace I could only now begin to appreciate. Here we sat sharing coffee and discussing Gary's departure like two good friends.

After a few minutes, I explained my dilemma to her; I did not want to tell her sons about their father's behavior. However, my counselor was adamant they be told in order to protect their own daughters. I explained the boys would probably view the information as a spiteful attempt to hurt them and their father, but it was corroborated as the truth. Liz asked about Kevin and what my plans were before she left.

I had difficulty believing her sincerity. I had put her in the same situation years earlier when Gary left her for me. She now empathized with me and wanted to make sure Kevin and I would be okay. She agreed to speak to her sons, but like myself, she could not guarantee their responses.

The following night, the phone rang. Gary's oldest son wanted to talk to Kevin. I promptly stepped out of the room, which allowed them complete freedom to talk. Kevin shared a small portion of the conversation with me. His half-brother had related Gary's explanation of the divorce. He told them you had kicked him out, for no reason. You kept all his pocket money and gave Gary no financial means. He also claimed all his wages went to pay our bills. Ellen graciously offered him a free room until he could get back on his feet. Kevin did not share anything else about the conversation, which had lasted for almost two hours. By the length, it must have contained much more information. I did not ask.

❦

For the first time in more than thirty years, I knew I was beginning to stand on solid ground. I began to look ahead with a new vision, a brand new start. The road would be bumpy. I had a lot of baggage, and the consequences for sin must be faced, even if we repent.

In the midst of this latest storm in my life, I was at peace, a tranquility with which I was unfamiliar. I read and, little by little, understood God's Word. As with a flower which has been transplanted and has to accommodate its new surroundings, God took root in my heart, and I learned He had a plan for me. Cautiously at first, but with growing conviction, I began looking to Him for my answers. In the center of all the mayhem, I was finding that which I had longed for, but from which I had run. God would walk with me through this long, lonely process before He showed me the place in which He had prepared for me to dwell, and just exactly where He could use me to His greater good.

But somehow, even before this was revealed to me, I knew that I knew that I knew down in my heart, God would work it out. I had, ever so timidly, begun to depend on my Creator for all the answers I needed. At that blossoming time in my life, I could never have fathomed what blessings God had planned for me.

Chapter Fourteen

After years of *doing it my way,* at long last I was returning back home. There was no epiphany; it was just little things at first. Each would ultimately begin to erode the long established, self-inflicted walls of isolation. These barriers would have to be obliterated beyond recognition to be free from all the history I had created. As they collapsed brick by brick, a new structure, fashioned of faith and built on a solid rock, rose up in its place. At the onset, finding truth in scripture, slowly but surely, I began to understand His love for me. I realized I could indeed trust Him, especially when I glanced back at the self-made desolation and wreckage I had just left. This new establishment still would not be easy to build as each brick was carefully put in place. At the time I had no idea it was preparation for an assignment; He had a plan for me.

Much like the prodigal's earthly father, my Heavenly Father ran to meet me: Throwing His gentle arms around my nagging loneliness, covering my open bleeding wounds with His all-healing royal robe of purple.

As with the kings and queens in history, who used a family insignia on a ring pressed into wax to authenticate ownership, my Heavenly Father's family insignia began to appear as an imprint on my broken heart, claiming me as His own. As so often happens in the midst of demolition, you cannot see the purpose amidst the confusion until the dust settles. It was not until later, looking back, I was to see how He was carefully destroying, deliberately, part of the defining structures in my life, so He could rebuild me in His image.

He reached out with His loving hands, took my weary ones, and led me through the next few months with such compassion. He disregarded all of my self-seeking history.

With the benefit of hindsight, I would see how God made my scant income stretch. In the wake of the facts, I should not have been able to pay all the obligations Gary had left behind; yet I did. I utilized the little savings of just a few hundred dollars. By watching our pennies, I was able to meet every single bill until the house sold. Where were those thousands I was accused of hiding? God knows I had none of the hidden assets I was *theorized* to have; I had something far better: GOD Himself. My lessons would come from Him:

> *I can do everything through Him who gives me strength.*
>
> *Philippians 4:13*

It was Saturday and Kevin had the day off. We viewed several local apartment complexes but nothing seemed right; always something was missing. Late that afternoon we found one particularly nice apartment which had all the things we had prayed together about, including their policy of accepting pets. Even Angel, our dog, would be able to remain a part of our family.

Our new home would be between our church, my work, and Kevin's school.

However, there were no known vacancies coming up in the near future. Still, the manager accepted my application to place on file. We were excited as we planned our future over a hamburger, fries, and soda before heading back to the house. It had not been a "home" for a long time, but we were filled with joy at the prospect of having one.

In the meantime, Gary had made it absolutely clear through a mutual friend, our marriage was over; he was not open to the idea of reconciliation. I accepted the news with greater ease than I had expected. Furthermore, he had no intentions of filing for the divorce. I would have to file because he could not afford the expense.

Within days and after prayer, I located a lawyer and began the process. I wanted to have a totally fresh new beginning, both physically as well as spiritually; I was so drained. I had learned this omnipotent God we serve is an amazing God of *new beginnings*.

We do not serve a God of second chances; no way! I am living walking proof of it. As a mere human, my *second chance* is blown before lunch daily. My heart's desire is: "*He must become greater; I must become less*" (John 3:30). As I looked back at my self-seeking life and all it held, I can only say a BIG, "AMEN!" Only with God's help can we have any hope of eternal peace.

⁂

On her previous visit, my realtor recommended a few repairs which, when finished, would increase value and appeal for the house. Again, the incomplete paneling on the wall in our family room was an example. Although Gary had been living in our house, his heart and mind had already moved next door. I smiled; thanks to the little confidence I was discovering, in Christ, I would never be alone again...never. This was one of many repairs which I could neither do, nor afford. God would have to provide.

As Christians, we often hear, "We are the hands and feet of Jesus." Our class at church stepped up in so many ways to prove that statement true. The men replaced the broken garbage disposal, installed the remaining paneling, replaced cabinet handles and completely groomed our yard. At the same time, the ladies began to pack up many items for the move which were unnecessary for daily life. Within a few days, the house was ready to be put on the market.

The realtors came on their house tour on Tuesday the following week. A lot of prayers went up: "Please let the house sell quickly and without any problems." The next Sunday when Kevin and I arrived home from church, we found our realtor in the hallway, wearing a huge smile on her face. She announced she had not one, but two full offers for the house. One of the offers was financially sound; there would be no difficulties with the sale. God had gone ahead. In my mind, I heard a crash, as another thick section of my old walls collapsed.

Overwhelmed with decisions and preparations for our new life, I began to claim the words of the song, "God Will Make A Way." Indeed, He was doing just that! I must have sung that song out loud or in my head over fifty times a day. It echoed in my shower, was heard inside my car as I drove to and from work and church. I hummed it as I shopped, cleaned, and lie in bed nightly; it was my way of holding onto a promise I did not understand. Yet I claimed in faith my Heavenly Father had a plan especially for me. It became my theme song for many months to come, shattering more of the walls I had built until they were almost nonexistent. I found myself beginning to learn more and more about the God from whom I had run. It felt so good, and an additional benefit was that I began to find value in myself!

On Monday I called the complex we had found. Much to my delight, I discovered an apartment would be available four days before we needed to vacate our house, and it was the very floor plan we had both wanted. Sing it over again. God had made a way! God also worked out a method of providing the deposit money for the apartment: I was allowed to take a portion of the escrow money from the sale of the house in order to secure our next home.

Five days later with checks in hand, I drove singing the song, "God Will Make A Way." Expectantly, I handed the clerk two checks (one, the deposit for the apartment, the other the deposit for Angel). As I did so, he remarked they had changed the rules: dogs were no longer allowed with new tenants. Tears sprang quickly, and I struggled to repress them. I explained I could not leave this canine behind. He was not just a dog...he was family.

Excusing himself for a couple minutes, he returned shortly stating, "The dogs which had already been here were grandfathered in, and if Kevin and you do not tell anyone, people will just assume you had moved in before the ruling took effect." He went on to add, "Because of that assumption, the two hundred dollar pet deposit will not be required." God had made a way again! Sing altogether now.

⊙⎯⎯⎯⎯⎯⎯⎯⊙

My only face-to-face encounter with Gary after his departure was a meeting to settle our finances, little as they were. We sat on opposite sides of this huge, long table, lines drawn and proverbial weapons ready, each with our own lawyers. Improbable as it seemed, our lives which were so intertwined at one time, so filled with potential, were now ending with us almost like complete strangers. In many ways, this man who sat across from me was just that—a stranger. Now we were reduced simply to hired counsels discussing the irrevocable decisions ending it all.

I had been required to produce, in advance, copies of statements to all bank accounts for the past four years. This meant piles of papers thanks to years of owning the trucking company. Compiling this information would have been prohibitively expensive had I not been a bank employee. What possible value did such an unwarranted request hold? Or was it a feeble attempt to find the elusive hidden treasure of eighty thousand dollars? I surmised it was one last chance to harass or intimidate me, but it was not successful. I was under God's covering now; He does not allow hate or bitterness, but only a servant's attitude.

Smiling slightly, I quietly told myself, *No animosity, or bitterness is worth the value I have discovered in being set free and given a new beginning.* As the meeting finished, Gary's lawyer offhandedly inquired about two savings accounts with a

125

balance of a little over one thousand dollars in each. I was totally unaware, as I had no thousand dollars anywhere anymore! Again, even with the perplexed look which must have been on my face, I flashed a friendly smile and responded. "Not mine, I can assure you!"

Two pages were pushed across the table at me as Gary inquired, "Then what are these?"

As I examined them, I was caught completely off guard. I stammered, "I don't know." One had Gary, Kevin, and my names attached; the other had my name, along with Kevin's, on the statement.

My face must have given me away, astonishment of the bombshell just dropped clearly written on it. Across the room, Gary's face displayed a smug look which said, "I gotcha."

I can only call it a God thing…. Suddenly, I remembered Kevin had a savings account for college. All of our names had originally been on the first account; the first balance statement he showed me. But Kevin had been concerned his father, whom he no longer trusted, might take it. I had moved the money to a new account to assure Kevin his college fund was safe. That was the second statement.

On explanation, I was challenged to prove it. I asked for the phone and dialed Kevin at his work. I outlined the scenario after alerting him he was on a speaker phone and who would be listening to his responses. Kevin interrupted me with the statement. "That's my college fund, and I moved it; my father can't be trusted. I can even recite the account number to you." Kevin was asked to give the numbers, twice, slowly, as the lawyer followed the numbers with his pencil on the statement. I turned back to the group to see Gary's eyes drop to his lap and a wave of his hand indicating it was over. Another unnerving scene of the movie was over as well.

⁂

We held a gigantic garage sale, netting over twenty five hundred dollars. For a second time my church family provided help, working until the sale was over and cleaned up. Afterwards,

I split the money and sent one-half of it to Gary. It was important to me to be honest with everything. I cheerfully gave him the odd penny.

On a later phone call, when he accused me of taking out wages for those who worked the sale for me, intimating nobody would help me for nothing, my conscience was clear. In fact, their pay consisted of a large lasagna, tossed salad and ice-cream bars. One very grateful hug and "Thank you," concluded the exchange of services.

Prudent advice given me by my godly counselor was, "Don't listen to your flesh, project yourself ten years out and don't do anything you will regret then." This astute pastor gave me some of the best advice I had ever been given. My prayer was I would be wise enough to put every bit of it into practice.

The walls I had surrounded myself with were toppling even more, and the fall was great. Soon they came tumbling down completely, much like the walls of Jericho.

⁘⁙⁘⁙⁘⁙⁘

On moving day, once again, our church family came to my rescue. As promised, at eight o'clock sharp, five pickups arrived, and, one by one, a load of our belongings drove away. Try as I might, I could not stop the tears as they stung my eyes and cascaded down my cheeks. "I'm just tired," I told the helpers as they walked in the room, but, of course, they knew different. This was the end. I thought I would never own a home, or get married again.

God had been true to His word. The church became His Spirit in human form. We had readied the house and gotten it sold. God *had* taken care of everything. Yet the void in my life felt so deep; I wondered if God could ever fix that too. At the same time, I was aware I did not deserve any of the blessings I was already receiving. God would fill the void! I was in preparation for what He wanted for my life. I was rather new at leaning on Him, but still confident, I could trust Him to make me complete. His word promised.

I remained behind to be sure the house was empty and ready for its new owners. After everyone left, I sat in the desolate family room, depleted of everything but the happy memories we had made there: The Sunday nights after church, while I popped bowl after bowl of buttered popcorn, watching Kevin and his friends and hearing, again, the laughter. The family all gathered on Christmas morning, in front of the crackling fire, getting our coffee while the kids impatiently squirmed for the gift opening to begin.

Glancing at the empty fireplace, I reminisced how thrilled I had been when we moved in. I had never had access to one before. I had used it as often as I could, and now, sadly enough, it would probably be my last. Still in all, I knew God, yet again, had met our needs.... Whom or what else did I need? It was one o'clock when I walked out of the house for the last time, leaving the keys resting neatly on the kitchen counter.

The amazing ladies from my church had also been Christ's hands and feet. While the men and I were at the old house, they were at my new apartment. They washed and filled the cupboards with dishes, set up furniture, put away the towels in the bathrooms, whatever was needed. By six o'clock that night, there were only two small boxes left to unpack to complete the move. Fresh flowers stood proudly on the table; the guest soaps rested in the decorative dishes; beds were made ready for us to fall into after an exhausting day. God had gone before me, and He had used my miraculous church family to do it.

God used those incredible people to show me what service and servant hood is all about. To qualify for service one must be knowledgeable of the problems. Well, I certainly was a specialist at sin but also equipped with proper tools to fix them. I was still learning, and the lessons continue even to this day. God always equips His children with the proper tools to accomplish His purpose. In this case, God's tools had been love, caring, five pickups, and willing hands to meet a deep need. In the months ahead, without any perception of it beginning, I, too, was trained to be a tool for His Kingdom.

The only need left in our lives was a vehicle for Kevin to drive for work and school. Gary had taken his truck and left only one car for Kevin and me. We both worked evenings and transportation often proved difficult. From my church, once more, came a blessing. Kevin could use an old beat up pickup which was on its last legs. It burnt almost as much oil as it did gas. But Kevin could use it until we found him a car. However, it was strictly for use between work and home. Willingly, we agreed.

Kevin and I had sat down together and built a list of the five most important things he wanted in his car. Faithfully, Kevin would eagerly search the daily paper. His anticipation showed as he read each and every advertisement seeking his very own car. Time after time, Kevin would find one, and time after time, my first question would be, "Does it have all five of the requirements?"

The answer was repeatedly a meek "No, but—" I told Kevin, we had asked, and God would provide in His time, not ours. We just needed to be patient.

What a transformation from the sad, hopeless woman I had been! Not long before I could never have envisioned words of that kind coming from me. I was now resting in the faith that God would take care of us.

Then came the call. A friend had found a car at an auction. It was perfect, but we would need to move quickly. It had every one of the five requirements and, in addition, an extremely expensive sound system. (Isn't that just like a father to give his son even more than he asked for?) The giddy look on Kevin's face, as he climbed behind the wheel with a huge smile and started his car for our new home, was unforgettable. God had become the Father of my fatherless son. Better yet, my son recognized His hand in it too.

Kevin had begun going to a Christian counselor almost immediately after Gary's departure. I wanted him to have every chance to understand and to overcome. It was a lot to get through, and I was not quite sure of the outcome. Losing your father, in such a haughty way, would be a tough challenge for anyone. He appeared to be doing fine: working with the youth on Wednesday nights, and attending services willingly, almost eagerly. His best buddies from church and school had been a great support for him as well. God was covering and protecting His child through it all.

Feeling a hand on my shoulder, I opened my eyes. "Excuse me again, ma'am, but we are about to land. Please put your seat up and be sure your seat belt is fastened for the landing." I followed her instructions; then impatiently waited for the time when I could continue the movie. But while I lingered, I mused about my life now....

His word says HE can use the broken. Only now did I realize how broken I truly had been. "He who began a good work in you will carry it on to completion until the day of Christ Jesus" (Philippians 1:6). He was directing my feet into unfamiliar territory. I had no way of knowing why He was doing all of this, but I was sure it was fitting into His plans.

After we landed, I went through the gate, scurried to the connecting flight and found my seat. This flight would complete the journey home. More than anticipating home, I was anxious to see the precious gift God had given me three years earlier. My godly husband, Doug, would be there waiting for me. I had told him the whole story before our marriage. He had still unconcernedly accepted my, "Yes, if you still want me" reply to his proposal of marriage. I could hardly wait to tell Doug the pieces of the puzzle God had shown me so we could speculate, together, about the outcome. God, with loving sensitivity, had to take me through one more hurdle, one more episode. For the remainder of the trip, He would re-run "the rest of the story." I smiled with excitement as I stepped back into the movie frames of my times past He was showing me....

⌘ *Chapter Fifteen* ⌘

The apartment seemed to give both Kevin and I a fresh, new-found start. Old memories had been left behind like those keys I had left on the kitchen counter at our old house. Our modest apartment became a home, filled with peace so long sought after. There was also laughter and senior teenage boys. From one meal to the next, I never knew how many people would be there. It was not uncommon for one particular boy, whose family was going through a bumpy time, to give us a call about dinnertime and offer to pick up something, if he could join us. On the weekends I could wake up to find as many as six boys, each with a blanket and pillow, sprawled out on my living room floor. Breakfast would always consist of cleaning out the refrigerator, sautéing all the leftovers together, stirring in a few scrambled eggs, putting the concoction between slices of bread, and calling them "The Famous McKevin Breakfast Sandwich." There was always one consistent request at breakfast: in unison, the boys would always remind me: "wait...don't forget the cheese!" This meal became a favorite, despite the fact the ingredients were always different.

We rented movies one winter night, and I prepared gourmet hot dogs, chips, and a potato salad. But the main attraction for the night was the huge snowball Kevin and I had rolled up to the patio edge. It must have been four feet high! As we were making the snowball, we had placed several six packs worth of soft drinks in it. So in order for the boys to get their drink, they had to "go fishing" for it. Life was good for both of us, and I realized as I watched the boys that night, my son was going to be fine.... God had revealed Himself to Kevin too. He had a Father, one he could trust, love, and emulate! His name is called God—the great "I AM" (Exodus 3:14).

With Christmas just days away, an envelope with Gary's handwriting arrived in our mailbox. Suddenly my mind shot back to the past and an unmistakable pain shot through my heart. My mind raced; what was he up to now?

When Kevin arrived home from work, I handed the letter to him. He, too, recognized the handwriting and just stood motionless for a moment.... "What do you think it is? What does he want?" He stood frozen as his eyes stared at the white envelope in his hand. I could see he, too, was replaying a past he was trying hard to put into its proper place. We both had stored the memories and hurt away so neatly in some recessed corner of our minds; this letter's appearance made those injuries leap into the present. Kevin was still seeing his therapist, and I suggested he talk it over with him. "But what do you think, Mom?"

"I think you have two options." It was a Hallmark envelope, so it probably was a Christmas card. Inside would undoubtedly hold a note and/or a check. I ticked off the options on my fingers as I listed them. "Option one: open it. You will need to establish if you want to respond to his card, and if you accept any money, you must send a thank you note. However," I cautioned, "should you open it, and then send it all back, he will probably assume it wasn't enough money. Option two: You can send it back, unopened, marked 'Return to sender', and you may never get another correspondence from him."

We both prayed right then for Kevin to have the wisdom to know what God wanted him to do. In his next session, the counselor gave Kevin the same advice. The envelope sat on the counter for about five days before Kevin picked it up, marked it "Return to sender" and dropped it into our mailbox.

"Are you comfortable with what you've done?" I asked.

"I don't need dad in my life, but I do need to let it all go," he replied. Then he added, "My counselor told me, 'you do not need a relationship with your father if you do not want one, but it is imperative you forgive him.'" Kevin wrote his father a letter shortly after the holidays. Basically it stated: he wished his father and Ellen the best, but had chosen not to have a relationship with them. He was letting go of the anger, as it was interfering with his walk with God. Kevin also wrote he realized since God was now the father he wanted to emulate, it was crucial not to damage that relationship.

Kevin has, by accident, seen his father twice: once in a store, the other time in the post office. Both times, Gary swore at Kevin and called him names. Kevin just walked away. Since then, we have both moved to a different state and there has been no communication between them for over ten years.

Chapter Sixteen

Although there was a superficial peace in our new life, in the background was an unexplainable heaviness lurking in my heart which I could not figure out. I avoided friends and acquaintances from church and work, at the grocery store, or other unexpected locations. I simply did not want to make small talk about how everything was fine or any other useless chatter. I only wanted to stay, as much as possible, by myself. *They* were all so cheery and seemed to always start the conversation with, "How are you?"

I just could not choke out the words, "Just fine, and you?" At one time, I had dreaded to be alone with myself, but now I craved it—perhaps a better word would be "required." I *required* my alone time. I did not need to pretend everything was okay when it was just me, but I would have to put on the endeavor of being happy in the presence of other people.

I would lie in bed counting the minutes until I had to leave. Ten more minutes, five more minutes, only two left, and at the very last second, I would hop into my clothes and arrive at work with just moments to spare before being tardy.

The front door seemed to become so heavy; my perception of this door was it weighed about two tons. I would often get ready to go somewhere, only to find myself unable to open it. The door in front of me protected me from the uncaring world outside and kept me safely sheltered. I had been so deeply hurt by interactions with other humans, being alone was now a sanctuary for me—not the seclusion it once had been. I just thought I was tired, and I attempted to ignore all the signs. I could not apply myself at work and my evenings were spent in bed, which provided a hiding place, even from Kevin.

One particular day at work I began to cry nonstop; the tears would not be staunched as they pelted down my face. Sobs were uncontrollable. It was as though an emotional dam had burst within me. There was a rushing flow of feelings which left me aching to find a hole, crawl into it, and pull the dirt in behind me—disappear and become invisible! To be totally undetectable.

Despite my resolve to stop the flood, tears spilled over, refusing restraint from my eyes. I locked up my desk, shut off my computer and told my supervisor, "Something is wrong. I need to go home, and I am not sure when I can get back." The supervisor looked up to ask why, but upon seeing my distress, she just advised I call her in a day or two. I barely waited for her approval as I headed out the door to deal with this latest surge of my past, now at the forefront of my mind. Why this? Why now, Lord? What is to be gained? I cannot change it!

In His loving way, God peels us like an onion. We find He takes us through correction and healing one layer at a time. With each layer, He reveals the next project He wants us to work on. Time after time, without exception, we have the choice of what to do with what He shows us.

I had buried some of my past, believing I was okay. But as I was about to discover, *okay* is not good enough for a daughter of the King. It was time to open the deep wound, riddled with the infection of guilt, and expose it to *The Son,* the true healing antiseptic of Christ's love. He restores what is broken.

As I headed for home, I was practical enough to know I was the only significant source of income in our household, and I could not take a chance of losing my job. With cascades of tears and heart-wrenching sobs I had no authority over, I drove directly to our family doctor's office. The receptionist took one look at me and hurriedly ushered me to the back into a small conference room. Before long the doctor arrived, dropping on the couch next to me, and placing his hand on my shoulder. "What's wrong, Kay? Talk to me."

Hysterically, the words tumbled off my lips, "I had an abortion. What kind of a woman kills her baby? I need help, please help me! Help me end this pain! Please!" I implored. The admission stunned even me; never before had I admitted to an abortion. Although I had locked the memories and guilt away deep in the vault of my mind and ignored them for years, I instinctively knew this was what God wanted me to resolve.

The doctor gazed directly into my eyes, and to my astonishment, there was no condemnation, no anger, simply alarm at my emotional state. "You're going to get a good Christian counselor, and I'll give you a prescription for a high dosage of antidepressants too. You'll be fine, trust me. We'll get you through this." He gently patted my shoulder to reinforce his edict.

Of all my sins, I believed most of them were forgivable—adultery, divorce, lying. But how could the killing of one's very own innocent child, who was safely tucked in my own body, ever be taken away? This might be the one exception God could not forget—or forgive. The one thing He would, and could, judge me on. I had absolutely no excuse, none which would clear me of the charge of murder I deserved.

"I had an abortion!" Those words, once verbalized, and the acknowledgement of what I had done, were the beginning of the transformation of Kay. In truth, I had three counselors and months of working through my life of sin. The adultery I committed with Gary was not, in my mind, the same as killing a pure guiltless baby, one of your own flesh. I had to work through my abortion before I could carry on my normal life activities.

Pastor Calvin began counseling me regularly, despite the fact he was dying of fourth stage cancer. Because of his concern for my welfare, not just for this world, but for my eternity, he gave me hours and hours of support—in God's Word. The condemnation I had believed I would receive from a minister for all my selfish transgressions was mute. I found him to be understanding, caring, and most importantly, armed with the Word of God.

One day during our time together, Pastor Calvin handed me a Bible. "Show me where it talks about big sin...little sin. Your belief appears to be some sins are forgivable while others are not. So, show me!" (There is no such reference or scripture to validate such a belief, yet many of us call this "truth.")

He then continued, "There are large rocks and small rocks, but the elements of which those rocks are composed of are the same. Sin is sin! It is sin anytime we break any of God's laws. Sin is sin! Only man makes a comparison because of the magnitude of the consequences our sins bring. Like rocks being thrown into water, man compares the size of the ripple rings and concludes the size of the sin. God does not differentiate. He simply states, He cannot abide sin." I sat speechless for a few minutes as he elaborated even further on his point.

When he had finished, for the first time I can remember, I began to understand. Tears came, yet again, from the depth of my soul at the truth of this statement. I began to understand what grace really meant. These tears were different than the others. These were of a meager understanding and unbelievable gratitude to a Heavenly Father who had, again, made a way for me. Only this time it was more than just a house sale or car. It was the knowledge that it was not the nails which held Jesus on the cross carrying out the sentence for my sins; it was His love for me. Even with all my faults, failures, and sins, HE had made a way for me to live with Him eternally.

I remember time and time again the pastor telling me Christ's blood had covered my abortion the first time I cried out with repentance, I was forgiven…even of an abortion. I would argue with him, "But you just don't seem to grasp what I am telling you. I cold-bloodedly had my child killed in the name of inconvenience! Don't you understand? Don't you get it?"

During one session, Pastor Calvin sat back in his chair, pushed himself away from the desk, and folded his arms. "Well, aren't you really the special one?"

"No!" I angrily fired back. "You just simply don't seem to get it; I killed her!"

Shaking his head with a gentle, caring smile on his face and love in his voice, he said, "No, Kay, *you* don't get it. You are sitting there telling me God sent His Son to die upon a cross for the sins of everyone in the world. Everyone, that is—but you? You're so special, you're telling God the gift of His Son is not enough! It's good enough for the rest of the entire world, but you're an exception!" It was like a cold washcloth slapped across my face. He got my attention.

Together we scoured the Bible for scriptures on how Jesus wanted me to look to Him, and what He could do with all my sordid past:

What has happened to me will turn out for my deliverance.

Philippians 1:19b

Undoubtedly the biggest obstacle for me...was me. To be given grace and mercy freely was beyond anything I could grasp. I had, for years, believed I was past any type of help. To accept mercy? Grace? Pastor Calvin suggested if I did not let Jesus take my sins and leave them on the cross, then I would be left to carry the burden of all I had done...alone. I had been doing that for years; I had no desire to remain where I had been for so long. I wanted a new fresh beginning, and this was my opening to get it.

I had not a clue how or where to begin. Pastor promised we would take it one step at a time. So we began, again, back into God's basic manual, the Bible (**B**asic **I**nstructions **B**efore **L**eaving **E**arth). First, we worked on what true repentance was from God's perspective. It was more than saying or being sorry. *Repentance* is meaning remorse from the depth of our soul and asking Him for forgiveness. We talked about true *repentance*, which is changing the pattern of our behavior to conform to His will. It is not what many use it for: asking forgiveness and then going right back to the same actions again and again. Forgiveness is not a free pass.

Second, we would discover *Mercy*. This gift is when we don't get what we deserve. I shuttered at what I deserved: I was an adulterer and a murderer. I had knowingly taken an innocent baby's life, hadn't I? How on earth could I expect anything else for myself but the ultimate of punishments? My actions warranted a death sentence; I should have been condemned. Instead, Jesus hung on His cross and stood between me and what I rightfully had earned. Because of His deep, profound love for me, I was shown *Mercy*. Now I was beginning to comprehend Jesus' sacrifice might just be enough for even me.

We need to be vigilant in what we advertise. Companies advertising their products give complete disclosure of possible side effects, for fear of being sued. As I look back over my self-absorbed life, I had advertised also. I advertised I was a Christian, proudly wearing the beautiful gold cross around my neck. I had quoted scripture as though I knew it, and lived by it, as well. I had been a hypocrite! Just like the Pharisees—proclaiming and displaying, HIS cross like a Christian, and actively living anything but a Christ-like life. God had ample grounds to condemn me, but instead HE chose to give me Mercy, to NOT give me what I deserved. I wonder now, with the mixed messages of a Christian example I was giving, what the people who watched me thought of Christianity because of my advertising.

I was now to learn and understand *Grace*. *Grace* means "receiving unmerited favor, that which I could never earn." *Grace* is an experience, not an idea or a concept. Once you recognize and have experienced it, you can never, never, ever be the same again. *Grace*, like *Mercy*, is a gift; it is free! I struggled to accept it was mine with no strings attached. How could God give me such a wonderful present? I did not deserve it.

Again, this godly pastor leaned across his desk to share some heavenly wisdom, "Kay—" looking directly into my eyes, "Kay, you're right, you don't deserve it. It's a gift—God's gift to each of us at no cost, just for the taking. All you need to do is reach out and grab it. Like any gift, we can do whatever we want with it. First option: take it, use it, and be grateful. Second option: put it on a shelf until a more convenient time. Last option: take it back to the giver and tell Him it isn't something you can use. Think about it. What's it going to be? I'll see you on Friday for your next appointment. You can give me your answer then."

I wanted *Grace*; I wanted it more than anything I had ever wanted before! If I could grasp *Mercy*, perhaps I could believe this too. I knew what I wanted to do, but my heart went faint with the thought of such a grandeur gift after such a haughty life.

Pastor Calvin informed me: Understanding those two things–*Mercy* and *Grace,* were vital for my complete healing, but the only way I would be able to receive them was by *Faith*:

> *Now faith is the substance of things hoped for,*
> *the evidence of things not seen.*
> *Hebrews 11:1, KJV*

Faith would be claiming my freedom from guilt, even when I did not *feel* it. It would prove imperative to disregard what my feelings told me, but to instead, depend wholly on His word. After a lifetime of going from highs to lows, ups to downs, I was now to depend on *Faith*?

Most of my adult life had been surrounded by fear: Fear I was not good enough, fear I would mess up again, fear someone would find out my secret. God led me to a passage showing me even David–whom God called "a man after my own heart" (Acts 13:22)–experienced fear:

> *When I am afraid, I will trust in you.*
> *Psalms 56:3*

Then, He showed me:

> *Surely God is my salvation; I will trust and not*
> *be afraid.*
> *Isaiah 12:2a*

In the first verse, fear came first, in the second, faith. I decided if I was to succeed, it would be in my best interest to have *faith* from the beginning; I had already had enough fear for a lifetime.

Once again, Pastor Calvin advised me, "What we feed will grow and what we starve will die." I had fed my fears of inadequacy for years. I could make a choice to now feed my *Faith* instead, to trust God's promises. Fear and faith cannot live in the same structure. One would be allowed to inhabit my mind; the other would need to vacate. I choose *Faith*!

Yet again, we began to wade through the scriptures on faith and what it had to offer me. I knew deep within me somewhere, faith was exactly what I needed and had desired with all my heart for years. I had looked everywhere else but where the answers lie—is with my Creator. Daily, I would have to renew the commitment I had made...trust God's Word and believe through faith.

Someone once said you cannot keep doing the same thing over and over and expect different results. It was time to turn from the old life which had brought nothing but disappointment and pain, and try something new. In my search for Christ, I had found what I had so longed for—**my value**. It promised to bring me peace from chaos, wholeness rather than brokenness, and an eternity of joy instead of constant strife. Being a stubborn German could now be my advantage. I needed to change; no—more than that, I *wanted* to change whatever it took. True repentance was working in my life and having visible effects. My next step would be to apply faith as well.

Applying it in my life...well, that was more difficult. I understood it in my head, but to imbed it in my heart provided a challenge. Many will tell you the hardest trip Christ ever took was the one to Calvary. I would suggest the hardest journey for humans is moving knowledge from the mental understanding in our brain (facts and figures) to the short twelve inches to our hearts. Truly believing it in the depths of our souls, where in a changed heart, understanding His love for us becomes real.

I began to read scriptures to reinforce my decisions. My faith started as the size of a small mustard seed, but as I fed it, slowly it grew. I realized the grip of fear I had carried for so long was ever so slowly beginning to lose its hold on me. The walls I had once placed so high around me were gone. Like a dry, thirsty sponge absorbing water, my faith absorbed the "Living Water" of Christ, and began to swell and grow. I basked in the discovery of my new beginning; I could hardly wait to get a chance to give away what I had just been given. Still, there were a few more steps I needed to learn and implement before I could begin effectively sharing my new path.

Pastor advised me: Forgiveness is a selfish thing. By forgiving, I would not be acknowledging those who hurt me were right. I would be saying, *I cannot change the past, and I will no longer allow it, or them, to control me.* Often those who have hurt us have moved on and forgotten; yet we carry the anger. So just exactly who was I hurting? We looked up numerous verses on forgiveness, and I began to realize, after all I had done, if I could be forgiven by Christ, to be totally free, I, too, would have to forgive.

I would argue with the pastor and justify my bitterness. He would bring me back to my own trespasses. Did I want them forgiven? Biblically, it was one of the prerequisites before my sins could be washed away, never to be remembered again. A hard assignment, but the outcome was to find my own release from the past. It was a slow, tedious process, but the more I gave up, the more I found a peace I could not explain.

After prayer, I believed God was requiring me to write both Jeff and Gary a letter of apology. (The appendices on page 207 contain the letters I wrote, as I wrote them.) Granted, they had done wrong by me, but when I stand before God one day, it will be my actions He will hold me accountable for...not theirs.

Gary's letter was my first step to yet more freedom and blessings. Our God always gives more than he requires. I prayed hard before and during that time, to say words which would effectively turn him to the Lord as well. Perhaps this would help him heal, if he had not already. Gary might be able to read in the letter what Christ had done for me and seek it for himself. The assignment was not easy or quickly accomplished. However, when it was completed, and a final prayer was whispered as it made a thump hitting the inside of the mailbox, I could almost hear more of the isolation walls crumbling.

I did not expect, nor receive, a response; I was happy without any correspondence with him. I simply prayed for him the same forgiveness I had found. Neither Kevin nor I desired to intrude on his life and have complete serenity with ours. I have no way of knowing what the letter did, or how it was received. I can only know the attitude with which it was sent and the prayers which went with it.

Like all of us, we make our own choices and will be held accountable for them. I was at peace; I had done what I was sure God had required of me. Forgiveness does not mean you need a relationship, it means letting go of your own control over the situation and letting God be in charge.

I actually spoke with Jeff at our granddaughter's graduation, telling him what I had done was very wrong. He had been unfair to me, yes, but he did not deserve the things I did to him. It was hard to face him and say those words, but I felt compelled to do so. Jeff's response was: He had a wonderful woman and a great life. I never received an acknowledgement of any of the injustices done to me. Surprising, even me, spiritually, I had come a long, long way, and I accepted his response with candor. He did, however, months after the graduation, ask for forgiveness from Suzie for his own behaviors directed at her. When she shared this with me, it was clear it had been immensely healing for her. Seeing the peace it brought her was an added and unexpected blessing for me.

Reflecting, I realized I had lost my freedom by my choices, instead putting myself inside impenetrable structures of guilt, misery, and bondage. I had denied His words of truth, whether it was deliberate or not, because to follow Him would limit what I wanted to do with my life. The pain I carried was so deep-seated, no human surgeon could possibly have cut deep enough to remove it. Instead, it would take the touch of the Almighty Healer and Physician, Jesus Christ, to remove the unrelenting pain of my sins.

I began to perceive surrendering to Christ was the most absolutely freeing thing I had ever done. There was no longer guilt; it was entirely absolved. No shame to be found in my heart; Christ had removed it *"as far as the East is from the West"* (Psalms 103:12). Having had no value in my previous life, I now found myself being called *"a pearl of great price"* (Matthew 13:46).

I had been broken beyond my own abilities to repair, but God says:

> *Therefore, if anyone is in Christ, he is a new creation; the old has gone, the new has come!*
> *2 Corinthians 5:17*

These things are available through Jesus Christ to anyone willing to repent and follow Him. The Bible says:

> *So if the Son sets you free, you will be free indeed.*
> *John 8:36*

To my astonishment, for the first time in my life, I *was* truly free. He was taking me to a place I never imagined I could go! He was taking my pain and reforming it into a passion within me. It was a burning desire to share my story—all my transgressions. That terrifying secret I had held as the ultimate anguish of discovery for so long, I could no longer keep contained. He would use me, and my story, for His kingdom.

Oh! I wanted to repay Him, but how? God does not *need* anything. What did I have which would be of value to Him? What could I give Him—the Creator of all things? The answer was clear and concise: He wanted me. With all my imperfections and flaws, He wanted me to be His child, to willingly and constantly commune with Him. In return, He would guide and protect me. That is what I can give Him.… My testimony could be used for His glory.

I could show others the gift of God's character. Forgiveness! Mercy! Grace! Love! I could share all I had done, how I had turned against Him, and then He turned it into something good. My life could be something to which others could relate.

Sin exists even in Christians. Shame is hidden deep inside people sitting next to you in the pews on Sunday morning. Brokenness is covered by a cheery, "Good morning!" They could realize they are not alone in the sea of humanity and be turned to God. Then they could also see what I had been given: a rich, full life built around Him. They may even achieve the joy my life has now. What a deal! My willingness was all He required, and I readily accepted the assignment.

Once you have been immersed in these magnificent gifts from God, once you understand, the sensation becomes like magma lying quietly at the bottom of a volcano. Then a reaction takes place. The magma begins to swell, slowly at first. Soon, it grows and expands. The pressure moves it toward the opening. With an explosive discharge, the magma spews into the air, landing on the surrounding area, leaving all that was there before, buried and dead. From the ashes of the lava, new, beautiful and rich life springs up.

Like a volcano, once we grasp what God offers each one of us, the reaction in our souls truly should make it impossible to keep the gifts to ourselves. Our spirits become rich and alive with His word. Like an eruption, the joy we find and the peace we receive demands to be shared with everyone around you. It becomes unbearable to contain it, compulsory to share. Some people may reject the news, laugh or disregard it. However, when someone (even one!) receives and accepts the good news, you will experience the most remarkable elation you will ever encounter.

If you are not giving it away, I would suggest perhaps you do not comprehend the enormity of the gift you have been given. And the strange thing about sharing, similar to the loaves and fishes which multiplied as Jesus fed the crowds (read the story in Matthew 14, Mark 6, Mark 8, Luke 9, and John 6), as you share, the passion and blessings multiply into larger quantities than when you began. There is an advertisement which says it best: "It is a gift which keeps on giving." That is my God!!! I had presented myself to Him as a broken offering, and He turned my life around and blessed me more than I could have ever dreamed. Oh, God, why did I wait so long to come to you?

One of the most significant, yet exceedingly difficult things, I had begun to learn was to practice to *"give thanks in all circumstances"* (I Thessalonians 5:18). This will take the rest of my life to master; to ignore those old feelings so easily rekindled, and walk by the newly found faith. Faith, I knew was required of me and of all who follow Him. His word says, *"Without faith it is impossible to please God"* (Hebrews 11:6). My years before this time had been a roller coaster, a long history of praising when things were good and questioning when things were not going my way. Now I was to speak praise in all things. I have greatly improved but have a long way to go.

I wanted to talk to Doug, to share what was happening, to incorporate him as part of this newly found life I knew I was being given. Oh, if I could only accurately express the joy! Everyone would run to it, but it is a choice and something no words this side of heaven will ever express adequately.

"Ma'am, can I offer you a tissue?" the lady in the seat beside me inquired. "You really look like you could use one." I had become so totally engrossed in what God was revealing to me, I

had been unaware of the tears which had escaped my eyes, wetting my cheeks, and flowing onto my jacket.

"Thank you, I'm fine. I'm just a little overwhelmed right now," I replied as I accepted the offered tissue. The weeping did not subside. How do you explain the amazing wealth God offers us so unreservedly when we come to Him? There will be tears in this lifetime; there are those of shame and sorrow. However, these were of overwhelming gratitude for the love to be found through Him.

I once heard a formula for figuring your true wealth: subtract everything from all you have which money can buy. Add everything death will not take away. Your true wealth is the result. "But store up for yourselves treasures in heaven, where moth and rust do not destroy, and where thieves do not break in and steal. For where your treasure is, there your heart will be also" (Matthew 6:20-21). I am indeed a very rich person.

I became aware of the airplane's motor backing off on power, and the sensation of slowing and dropping as we prepared for landing. Just seconds later, the lights came on and a voice over the speaker verified we were in our approach decent and about to land. As the movie came to an end, I was aware this storyline was far from over. This lengthy journey was about to end, but a more exciting sequel loomed ahead....

Service

Chapter Seventeen

I began reapplying my now worn and almost non-existent makeup. Dabbing the last of the moisture from my eyes, I touched up my mascara, clearing away the smeared mess of tear tracks down my cheeks; then, applied a hint of lipstick. I wanted to look my best for Doug. He always looks handsome without even trying, one of his many great attributes. I had truly gotten God's best when he brought us together.

I smile as a verse flashes through my mind:

> *Do not be yoked together with unbelievers.*
> *2 Corinthians 6:14a*

Why did I not do it His way all along? I was only kidding myself when I thought I knew how to live my life! I would not have caused the road of destroyed marriages, the line of injured people, or the damaged children if I had heeded God's ways throughout my years. Living with my feet firmly planted on the path God had chosen for me is so much better a life than I had ever imagined.

Contemplating, I find myself torn. If I could go back and change it, would I? Without my past, would I have my life today? Would I be without His forgiveness? Is not my past a part of who I am, and what I have become? If possible, I would retract all the pain I caused others in a minute. Having my aborted child to hold, grandchildren from that child, would be my heart's desire.

The question is: What would I be? How much less complicated my life would have been without my stubborn sins. The best way is to cling to Christ and follow Him from the very beginning.

As I was finishing my facial restoration, the lady seated next to me began, "Do you travel much?" I shook my head, hoping to not have to engage in conversation, though I think she was trying to be sure I was okay after all the tears. "Well, last year my husband and I went to England and had a wonderful time. For our next vacation, we will have to build stamina. It will be a long, hard trip just to get there. This coming year we are headed for Australia."

What?!? Had I heard her correctly? Had she just confirmed another piece of the puzzle? That was the very word, "stamina," which had been given to me while on my knees with Cindy less than twenty-four hours ago. Still, with all the interim events, it seemed like twenty-four years. Having traveled through all the years and sins of my past, it felt more like an eternity.

Then her last sentence penetrated my consciousness— Australia. Is it another link? A couple days earlier, I had met a lady from Down Under. She had been persistent in asking me questions. The following day we met again for coffee. It was a three-hour meeting which ended in her question. "Would you consider coming on a tour to Australia if I set it up?"

It almost took my breath away as I answered, "Well, God would have to provide the finances, but I would be thrilled to come." We had exchanged information and parted with a promise of keeping in touch.

There are no coincidences with our God. The seldom used word, "stamina," had been used by two separate people in less than twenty four hours. Also, two trips to Australia were mentioned in the same short time span. My heart raced in apprehension; God was moving in my life. What did He have planned?

"Oh, my!" the lady next to me was speaking. "Did I say something to upset you? I didn't mean to make you cry again!"

"No," I explained, "I think you just confirmed something for me, and I am just overcome with joy." Imagine! God sending me to Australia—a country everyone seems to want to visit—halfway around the world from my hometown. It was a place I had only read about in books and wondered at its beauty and attractions! I gave up on restoring my makeup, as the gentle tears began trickling down again; Doug had seen me in worse shape. He would still love me, even on my worst hair or make-up day.

The plane came to a halt, and within a few minutes, we had taxied up to the gate. Everyone rushed to gather their belongings. Grabbing my carry-on bag, I realized, perhaps, I would be packing and repacking my bag to serve the One who saved me. Not in my wildest dreams could I comprehend the real journey which was being launched.

I hurriedly disembarked and scurried to the terminal exit. There he was—Doug! His arms filled with red roses and a huge smile on his face. I practically knocked him down as I rushed into his strong arms. After a kiss, I began to spew the last forty-eight hours of events, trying to fit it into forty-eight seconds. "Slow down, Honey, slow down! You just got home; we have plenty of time to talk!" Doug tried to staunch my informational flow. But I was not to be slowed. The prayer with Cindy, the promise, and the movie I had just seen—all of it! He needed to hear all of it! I just knew that Doug, too, would be astonished with the news summary which was pouring out of me.

It was a first, but my luggage arrived at the baggage claim before we did. Doug grabbed my large bag as I continued to rattle all I wanted to share. As we headed to our car, Doug tugged my suitcase behind him, smiling, as I incessantly poured out all the events and the inescapable design, I believed, God had something in mind for my life.

When I finally stopped to catch my breath, Doug simply said, "Well, if God has this journey for you, you have my full support. Just do whatever it is you're being called to, Honey. I'll be right by your side. I hope you know that."

When we climbed into our car, the baggage now tucked in the trunk, both of us sat stunned, rather speechless at what all these occurrences seem to suggest. Whatever it was, we agreed, we would be in it together, just as we did everything else in our marriage. He reached over and patted my hands, now resting in my lap, and started the car for home. We sat in total silence for a while as though we both were trying to comprehend it all. Home loomed ahead when we next spoke and began to second guess what all the signals might imply, and how we would respond to His will and desire for us.

⁜

It was a couple nights later: I was awakened by the presence of the Lord upon me. It was like being on a stage with the beaming brilliance of a spotlight directed straight at me. I was so overcome with awe; I slipped from the bed and lay prostrate on the floor. I remember whispering in astonishment, "Just use me, Lord. Just use me. I will take this journey as you disclose it to me. I just want to be an instrument you can use." I do not know how long I lay there. The warmth and peace were so heavenly I never wanted to leave. I had made a pledge to follow the Lord's path before, but the personal encounter with God sealed my resolve.

The next day over coffee, I shared the previous night's visitation and my resolved promise with Doug. Something big was about to burst, and I was confident the "journey" must include Australia. The puzzle was almost complete, yet it was so far beyond my comprehension. I struggled to find faith in what I was seeing, hearing, and feeling.

⁜

God's plan is intricate and divine! Soon after His visit, I spoke with a real estate agent, Lisa, about renting a vacation home. During the conversation I asked if pets were allowed. I told her mine often were my traveling companions when Doug could not accompany me and had been trained as therapy dogs for hospitals, cancer centers, and rest homes. She caught the past tense of the statement and asked what I did now. After taking a breath and trusting God to give me courage, I shared, "God has given me a ministry, but it is still in the infant stages. I have given my testimony only a couple times." Lisa asked my subject. My response was, "Abortion." All noise stopped.... The phone appeared to have gone dead.... "Hello? Hello, are you there?"

It was a few seconds before I heard a soft voice. "You talk about it?" Recognizing the pain wrapped in the folds of her astonishment, I suggested we might meet for lunch. She readily agreed.

I drove to a small country restaurant about 25 miles away, to find Lisa waiting inside. I brought her a book on abortion recovery, which she gratefully accepted and quietly slipped into her purse. Over a simple sandwich plate, I shared my recent trip and experience, but also that I was not sure of the extent of its meaning yet. It quickly became apparent she had a warm friendly spirit despite the deep hurt of her abortion.

In an effort to restore herself to complete health, she agreed to begin a healing Bible study with me. We set a time and date for me to meet her at her home for the first session. I paid the bill, and as I turned to leave, there was Lisa, standing almost face-to-face with me.

"How much does it cost to go to Australia?" she inquired.

I replied, "I am not sure I'm going yet, but I did check prices earlier. It is about one thousand two hundred dollars, round trip."

Lisa cut right in, "How soon do you need it? Is a week too long?" Again, I explained I was still not even sure I was to go. "Well," she said very determinedly, "I'll have your money in a week. Is that okay?" I reiterated the fact I was not sure the trip was truly God's plan. She might also want to think about it, and speak with her husband concerning the amount of money. "No! No! I heard God speak to me as clearly as I hear you now! I am to pay your way. I have the ability, and the desire; you'll have your money in a week. Okay?"

I really do not remember too much after that; I was so dumbfounded. I think I mumbled a belated, "Thank you," as she walked to her car and drove away. It took me several minutes to recapture my composure. Once I did, I was on the phone to Doug and then to our pastor.

It was difficult to fathom! God's planned journey was a trip to Australia. He had woven a series of unrelated incidents: a March for Life I had secretly attended and a family vacation. And arbitrary people: an "Auzzy," an airplane seat neighbor, and a real estate agent, together, to make His determined path clear!

Chapter Eighteen

I had only spoken my testimony a couple of times prior to going to the March for Life in Washington D.C. Before I could share with any more strangers, I had to tell my kids. I feared their reactions. They could walk away, reject me; they might not be pleased with public speaking about such an unwelcome subject. But their reactions would be much worse if they heard what I was doing from someone else. No matter how hard it would be, my children deserved to hear my testimony, first-hand—now.

Whatever reactions I received from my children, I had heard the call of my Savior, given my oath to go where He would send me, and I knew He was calling me to make public appeals for His sake. This was, beyond a doubt, the most difficult thing I had ever had on my to-do list, but it needed to be done.

I asked Doug, our pastor, and a couple close friends to be in prayer; the outcome could be catastrophic. I recited to myself the "fear not" promises from the Bible I had memorized for times like these. I also began to sing my old theme song again, "God Will Make A Way." I prayed as I drove to DeeDee's home, "God please! Do not let this destroy my family."

Since DeeDee and her family lived in a different state, I planned a whole weekend to go see her. I arrived Friday night after everyone had already gone to bed. When she greeted me at the door, DeeDee gave me a huge hug. I could not help but wonder if she would still want to support me when I left, or if she would ever invite me to return. Faith—now is when I would need and use my faith.

We sat in a dimly lit room, with only the bright embers of the fireplace cutting into the darkness. *The shadows will protect me from the look on her face when she hears the news,* I encouraged myself. I knew it was time to stop making small talk when my stomach made a huge leap, turning into a gigantic knot. "I have to tell you something, DeeDee, and I am not sure you're going to like what I have to say." My throat tightened, and my heart raced.

"You know I love ya, Mom! Let's hear it," she quickly responded. My eyes welled with tears, wondering if she would feel the same way in five minutes, or would I be heading for a long, solitary drive home soon?

Abruptly, I dropped the bombshell, "I had an abortion, DeeDee. Before Kevin, I selfishly had an abortion." Deep-seated sobs came from inside me. "It's been a secret for all these years, but I have finally dealt with what I did. I've had intensive counseling, and I understand now God has forgiven me." I took a deep breath as I continued, "You girls took the brunt of much of my guilt. I killed one daughter; how could I love and hug the other two? I did not mean to push you away; I did the best I could with all the guilt I carried. I am so sorry for the hurt I caused you both." I am not sure exactly what else I said as I rattled on for several minutes and poured out my heart to her. Then gathering every ounce of faith and courage there was within me, taking a deep breath, I asked meekly, "Can you forgive me?"

Then came her soft voice, "Mom, Suzie and I figured it out a long time ago, and there is nothing to forgive."

I had been free once I realized God had forgiven me, but the forgiveness of my youngest daughter gave me renewed strength to finish my disclosure. How would she feel about the rest? "There's more," I began; DeeDee looked at me expectantly. "I think God is calling me to speak publicly about it, to speak about the repercussions of the guilt, and also His transforming grace. He has made a way and provided an opportunity to share in a couple weeks. But I felt I needed to speak to you kids first." There was a hesitation, and my heart sank. The silence was deafening and seemed to last an eternity. As if she could not find sufficient words, she simply gave me the biggest, best hug I had ever received.

DeeDee began to enlighten me on some of the little slips which she and Suzie had noticed. One of the things she said, I had completely forgotten in all my years of pretending nothing had happened. Suzie had approached me one day years ago when Kevin was still very small. She tried to tell me God had revealed to her a secret I was carrying. When she spoke the word "abortion," I was horror-struck. What kind of God would divulge that to my daughter? I called her some pretty heartless names and denied her "vision." We never spoke of it again. By no means did it cross my mind that Suzie would share such a deadly secret with DeeDee. In the interim, they had gotten together and both girls knew my deepest and darkest secret. Amazing actress I believed I was; I had not been as great as I thought.

What she said next was beyond anything I hoped for or dared to consider. "Mom, can I be your first prayer partner? I'll be on my knees when you are on the stage. I love you!" I reached out once again to my wise and loving daughter. Tears and more tears gushed while we embraced, as did my gratitude to a Savior who had gone before me and made His way.

Upon returning home, I called Suzie because she was too far away to visit in person. When I broached the subject and shared what path God was calling me to, she was also forgiving. Being the oldest, she bore more of my anger and indifference than her siblings. Yet she, too, was willing to let the past go. Suzie was more sympathetic than I could ever have imagined. She offered to pray with me before I spoke and wanted to be the first to hear the results of my testimony. "I am proud of you, Mom, really proud!" were her exact words. Somewhere, somehow, I must have done something right.

I was two-thirds of the way through my biggest life challenge. However, there was still one more test, the most sensitive one yet. I needed to face Kevin—my miracle child. Contrary to saving the best for last, I had saved the hardest until the end. Being "single together," as we had called it, going through tough times simultaneously, we developed a very close relationship. I had always vowed to be a good mother; now that carefully crafted image was about to be utterly destroyed.

Kevin was now married. Not quite a year after my own wedding to Doug, I found myself helping Kevin plan a wedding ceremony to a beautiful, Christian girl from college—Madeline. The big day arrived, and I watched my baby boy, once so utterly downcast, stand with his head held high, expectantly looking down the aisle. A handsome young man in his own right, who had overcome so much, was now taking a wife himself.

The reception after the ceremony brought a flashback of our past. It is a memory which will never fade. After the first dance, true to tradition—the bride with her father, it was our turn, mother and son. We took the dance floor. As we dipped and swayed to the music, he looked down at me and asked with a smile, "Mom, what are you thinking?"

Surges of unexplainable pride swelled within me as I responded, "I was thinking of the broken teen who once told me, 'Mom, I will never get married, never! I will never allow anyone to get close enough to me to hurt me the way Dad did you.' And here you are today, beginning a new family of your own. Where once you were filled with doubts and insecurity, now you stand whole and completely restored, thanks to Jesus."

Smiling sadly as I remembered the episode, I wondered if his healing was complete enough to cover the most serious of my transgressions. Could he, too, forgive me as the girls had done? I would need to make one more trip; I prepared to visit them. *Jesus, please, give me courage greater than my own to tell my son about his mother's past. I simply can't do this alone! Please, God, come with me.*

I had been given two forgiven judgments by my daughters. Now I was pleading for one more, just one more. I needed the forgiveness from Kevin, the boy who had suffered the most at the hands of his parents. We had always discussed everything, now I would tear the image of a good mom into shreds by my announcement. *Father, I ask for just one more person granting me forgiveness. I can take the pain of the world's revulsion towards me, but I beg you, not from Kevin. Father, not Kevin!*

I arrived on their doorstep filled with uncertainty; I panicked at what the outcome of exposing my secret could be. After dinner we sat in the living room to chat. *Now! Tell him now!* The lump in my throat and the pounding of my heart had to be enough to give away my apprehension. I opened my mouth to confess...and was interrupted by the doorbell. It was Madeline's parents dropping in, bringing a delicious lemon pie with them. It was a nice surprise and a pleasant evening, but such timing!

Later, after her parents left, my courage fled. I reasoned it was too late; I would tell them tomorrow. I knew there were people praying right this minute, but their prayers would still be good in the morning. Wishing them a good night, I headed for my bedroom. I brushed my teeth, got into my pajamas, and started to crawl into bed. But God's timing is always perfect, and not necessarily the same as mine. In my heart I heard Him say: *Now!* Slowly, I walked down the hall and tapped lightly on their door. Perhaps they were already asleep, or maybe one of them was in the shower. When they answered, I asked them to step out; I needed to share something important with them.

Madeline and Kevin sat on a couch directly across from me as I sat on the edge of their new beige rocker. *Here we go, Father, my precious son and his brand new wife. Be gracious to me one more time. Remember when you gave up Your Son? Please, I don't want to lose mine.* As I had done before with DeeDee and Suzie, I slowly began sharing the true purpose of my visit, including what I believed were God's intentions for my life. As I got to the part about the abortion, I could not bring myself to look directly at them; I could not bear it if my son showed his utter loathing for his mother when shown in the worst light. As an alternative, I stared down at their heritage blue carpet, as afraid as I had ever been, my new-found faith wavering in the silence. Through tear-filled eyes, I saw two sets of bare feet running across the beautiful blue carpet, and immediately found myself encased in a group bear-hug.

Through tears of their own, they began to encourage me. Kevin stepped back, and with a sigh said, "Mom, it's okay. You know when Dad left, you did all you could to give me stability. But, well, I did some things myself." My belief that my son, with his counseling and close relationships with the boys in his church youth group, had avoided any real stumbling blocks was shattered. In shear bewilderment, I listened while he explained. Unbeknownst to me, he had exhibited some pretty unacceptable behaviors. Kevin then assured me he had asked forgiveness and was, again, walking the path with God I believed he never left. Not wanting to hurt or disappoint me, he carried his own dark secrets.

God was not through with me yet! Madeline began, softly at first, sharing a secret as well. She had her own regretful actions which caused her to stumble in her walk. She clarified, however, neither she nor Kevin had kept secrets from the other before their marriage. "Seems we each have a history. We've all done things against God we're not proud of. So, Biblically, how can we hold anything against you?" she asked through her tumult of tears.

We all chuckled in a nervous way at the deceptions we each carried out but had now exposed to one another. The dreaded night ended so differently than I had projected, concluding with the three of us on our knees in the middle of their living room, all praising the Lord. There were tears, smiles, and giggles as we realized what had just occurred. We prayed together and thanked Jesus for the cross and His blood which covered us all. What the enemy had planned to exploit, to destroy my family, God had used to unite and knit us together as never before. It was a night which will long be remembered, one which changed us all. Praise God! There was a huge community hug as Kevin ended the evening with "Go get 'em Mom! You have our blessing."

It was two o'clock in the morning by the time we went back to bed, but I used my cell phone to call Doug once I was back in my room. I just could not wait until the light of the next morning to share such exceptional news! So typical of Doug, he was still up, praying and hoping to hear the outcome. He was caught speechless with wonder as I shared the joyous events of the night. "We truly serve one indescribable God, don't we, Honey?" Late as it was, he wanted, and seemed to hang on to, every single detail I could remember. "I am so glad it all came together. I know God has plans for you, and I was sure He would work it out, one way or another." We said our goodnights with a promise of a new day tomorrow and a trip back home.

❦

One of the last steps in my healing was to name my baby. At the time of the abortion, I was in no condition to ask, nor did I ever discover, whether or not I had a son or a daughter. However, when I cried out with a sorrowful heart, I shrieked, "I killed *her*!" After many hours of prayer, I felt God confirm my aborted child was a daughter. We girls (DeeDee, Suzie, Madeline, and myself) held a barrage of phone calls in order to name her. Her name is Sara Marie.

With the support of my family, and the terror of *discovery* missing from my heart, God was ready to MOVE my ministry. This omnipotent God, from whom I spent years running, was now taking the most dire thing I have ever done—killed my own child—and in His providence, was turning my misery into a ministry. Who better to understand how a woman feels when she is condemned by her own choices but someone who had walked the same lonely path? Someone who had, like myself, felt the excruciating pain and finally come to merciful healing, bringing wholeness! It would require a kind of courage only God could provide. But He could give me the audacity to share with strangers, whose disdain would be far less devastating than anything I might have experienced if my family rejected my message. Within a very short time, God would prove His ideas to be more grand and far-reaching than my limited vision could imagine.

The first thing God did was to lead me to a scripture to represent the ministry:

However, I consider my life worth nothing to me, if only I may finish the race and complete the task the Lord Jesus has given me—the task of testifying to the gospel of God's grace.

Acts 20:24

Quoting the Apostle Paul, Luke summed up the unbelievable call to service I had been assigned. Imagine, me talking about how God's grace covered my abortion to perhaps hundreds of people! How would they respond? How would my close friends react? These are people who thought they knew me, but from whom I kept this hideous secret. Then I remembered my scripture. My task was not to make friends or answer to them. As much as I loved my long-time associates and wanted them to accept my story, this journey was more important. I would gladly accept worldly rejection in order to not intentionally let my Lord down again. I owed Him too much.

I had once again given God a solemn and unconditional vow: I would follow where He leads. Just as when God granted me Kevin, I was determined to do everything within my abilities to make sure I kept my promise. As the realization of task requirements dawned, I understood it would have to be in His ability that I carried through my guarantee; my knees went limp at just the thought of standing before others and pouring out the secret which had held me captive for so long, which had at one time shattered my life.

Sara Marie was never given a chance to feel the sunshine on her face or to shyly hold a boy's hand. However, my friends and family agreed her memory would now live on in this ministry. Then God showed me, once again, His hands were holding this ministry and molding it to His desires. My scripture verse called me to share my testimony and demonstrate God's grace.

Through that marvelous grace, a person could be restored to full life and healed of their deepest wounds. I was **S**haring **A**gain and **R**estoring **A**nother, which was exactly my calling. So, Remembering S.A.R.A. Ministries International officially began in April 2004. The name of my ministry would both honor Sara and reflect my commission.

❧❧❧❧❧

The minister from the church where Doug and I are now actively attending, Pastor Randy surprised me! He not only supported my ministry, which features a taboo subject, but also suggested I extend the ministry from the church. There would be many benefits to come from this suggestion. All monetary donations to Remembering S.A.R.A. Ministries International could now be considered a charitable donation under the 501-C3 tax status. This ministry, in its infancy, would have a home church, a body of believers who would pray for the outreach and give encouragement to Remembering S.A.R.A. Ministries International. This pastor is wise *and* has a business sense.

Pastor Randy's next recommendation was to form an accountability team. The purpose of this team is to pray about opportunities which materialize. The direction and decisions made for the ministry would not be fully reliant upon only one person. After spending time in prayer individually, asking God's guidance, should one of the team members feel uncomfortable about an appointment, then I would not accept the assignment.

Pastor Randy was adamant about accountability! He assured me he, personally, had no questions about my integrity, but this team of prayer warriors would protect me from any accusations or questions of impropriety. Through the intervening years, my accountability team has been a blessing. One of the places I have always wanted to work is in Africa because of the great need found there. Although I have received some invitations, my team does not feel I have been called to Africa. I believe God has not said, "No!" But instead, has just said, "Not yet." But in either answer, He knows best. Pastor's wisdom has been a shield of protection against someone who would challenge the credibility of this ministry.

He extended support in an arena and subject from which I would discover many churches would cower. Sadly, I would encounter many churches that would choose not to get involved in the controversial subject of abortion. Their excuses: "It is too political," or "We can't bring up something so personal in church." It is as if the scriptures like, *"Thou shalt not kill"* (Exodus 20:13, KJV) and *"Before I formed you in the womb I knew you"* (Jeremiah 1:5), and *"I set before you life and death...choose life, so that you and your children may live"* (Deuteronomy 30:19) have been eradicated from their Bibles. This is a purposeful choice of the body of Christ to remain silent, to turn aside and ignore the pain of so many in the name of political correctness.

What? The church was created to be a safe place for any and all who need spiritual healing for whatever reason. Where else will the congregation hear a healing message? Who else will assure them they can receive forgiveness? Cringing behind their sin, without hope, many women today still believe they have committed an unforgiveable sin. The silent belief is: if it cannot be spoken of in church, then indeed, it must be horrendous and beyond redemption. Wrong! Wrong! Wrong! Praise God His Son's sacrifice can cover **ANY** sin, with the proper repentance. It is tragic for the church to remain silent, while holding the answer. God forgive them!

❦

My head spun for the next few days in bewilderment as things rapidly fell into place. Lisa's check arrived, just as promised. I now had the funds to travel to Australia. The lady from Down Under confirmed they could fill a full five weeks of engagements, then asked, "Do you have any interest in going to New Zealand for an additional week?" Already, this ministry was extending beyond the borders I thought God had in mind.

Doug believed, although we did not have the resources, that he was to accompany me on the beginning Remembering S.A.R.A. Ministries International trip. So he stepped out in faith, updated his passport, and got the required immunizations with me. Just one month before our departure date, an anonymous donation was deposited into my new ministry account; it contained a note, "For Doug to accompany Kay to Australia." Now he would be able to join me on the first of the many breathtaking journeys.

My human view of God and His power and His might is so minuscule in comparison to His reality. Doug suggested I needed an email address and business cards for Remembering S.A.R.A. Ministries International; I declined. Someone else thought a website or blog would be a great asset; I chuckled and brushed off the proposition. One day Doug, perhaps tired of my small ideas, put international calling on my cell phone. I believed he was rather idealistic and imaginative! Pastor Randy told me one day I would write a book. Where do these people come up with this stuff? My vision was so short sighted, yet despite my limitations, my God is SO BIG! He will take and use this ministry as He has planned, not as I restricted.

◦◦◦◦◦◦◦◦

Our lives are like jigsaw puzzles, often most like the ones which are peculiarly shaped. Some pieces have familiar definition, while others are individually distinctive and difficult to determine their correct places in the overall image. Most people begin by assembling the edge pieces of the picture, joining them to form a frame, giving the puzzle boundaries. God arranges our lives in a similar fashion, allotting parameters within which to live—not to keep us prisoners, but to protect us. When we allow Him to, He ever-so-lovingly adds some of the center pieces to enhance the richness—the fullness of our lives. This is always done in His perfect timing and way. The methods the Lord uses never seem to be what I think they will be and are always somewhat extraordinary and unique. However, with each piece placed, the picture becomes more beautiful, closer to what the artist intended.

Of one thing I am sure, there is one piece in each of our puzzles which is specifically created and fashioned to be filled only by our Savior, and by Him alone. Many people try to fill the need with drugs, alcohol, and self-seeking pleasures, only to discover that place is still empty and void of that which we were seeking—happiness and true peace. There is only One who is capable of filling it wholly—Jesus Christ.

What happens when we wander outside the limits? He still loves us! When the pieces of our individual puzzle appear jumbled, and seem to have no pattern or purpose because of our decisions, our God is not taken by surprise. Nor is He wondering what to do next. We can take assurance in the fact He never gives up on us. His word says:

He who began a good work in you will carry it
on to completion until the day of Christ Jesus.
Philippians 1:6

We will only be complete on Judgment Day when we stand before Him. At that point He will say either, "*I never knew you. Away from me*" (Matthew 7:23) or "*Well done, good and faithful servant*" (Matthew 25:21). I can imagine our individual puzzles will appear like a mosaic from His view. Each of us will be shown as a beautiful, precisely placed picture inside the whole montage. I truly doubt any of us will care then. We will be too in awe of Him.

◈ *Chapter Nineteen* ◈

There is one very rewarding responsibility for which God has repeatedly used me, improbable as it is because of my own inadequacies; I find myself as a counselor. I have the privilege of watching people who were bound in endless chains finally being set free as they hear and accept the truth about our merciful God. Their acceptance brings me great joy because I have been there! I can understand the feeling of being hopeless and experiencing the release of guilt. I know, personally, what God is capable of doing when we allow Him to work in our lives and am honored for even a small part of the journey which allows these individuals to rise up and stand tall in His strength.

What about you? What about your secret? Does it still bind you? Have you placed it under the blood of Christ, beyond any doubt? Or are you still in some way caught in the web of lies spun by the enemy? Do you have a true and intimate relationship with Jesus Christ? He is the only way; there is no other!

> *I am the way and the truth and the life. No one comes to the Father except through me.*
>
> *John 14:6*

I have been asked, "Be honest with me. Do I qualify for this grace and the resulting forgiveness?" If you are a sinner—congratulations—you qualify! The Bible clearly states who the sinners are:

For all have sinned and fall short of the glory of God.

> *Romans 3:23*

Each one of us is a sinner and His grace is available to cover every transgression:

My grace is sufficient for you, for my power is made perfect in weakness.

> *2 Corinthians 12:9a*

God promised us in Isaiah 55:11 that His Word will never return void! The Bible also tells us God cannot lie (Numbers 23:19). So, you too can be free!

I often hear, "But I don't deserve it!" To which I readily agree. No human does. Still, God has made it available at absolutely no cost, just for your taking. Gifts of great value are always the most difficult to accept. It is like having your house mortgage paid in full by another person. When going to the mortgage company and attempting to make a payment, if there is no balance due, the mortgage company does not know what to do with your disbursement because the liability is no longer on the record. Someone has already paid your entire, well-deserved debt balance for you. His name is Jesus Christ, God's only Son! The record of your past iniquities has been purged from God's book.

Even after accepting the gifts of grace and mercy, the enemy will still try to whisper in your ear. He will attack you when you are most vulnerable. The place he targets is different for each person, but has one thing in common among all people: It will be the point on which he has won past battles with you. He will try to convince you nothing has changed; you are still lost. Satan can even make you *feel* valueless, but remember, God tells us we cannot depend on our feelings. Do not be intimidated by your past; have faith. Instead, boldly remind Satan of his future.

Counseling is a great responsibility as well as a privilege. Bathing it in prayer, continuously asking for wisdom, and studying the Word for accuracy, are all emphatically required. I never treat any subject flippantly. It is my honor for someone to entrust me with their very deepest hurts and pain, one which requires absolute confidentiality. I assure them, unless required to tell the authorities by law, no other person will ever hear their secrets from me. They need to feel they have a safe place to share, where they will not be criticized or judged. Each story is unique, yet there are common threads.

Too often I hear, "But this is not the entire story; you don't know what else I've done!" Jesus covered every one of our past sins with His blood and stands before God on our behalf. Confess those sins, all of them, and He will give you a new beginning in Him.

Another person wails, "I don't have any talents! What can I do?" Every single person, without exception, has a God-given talent. These unique qualities were placed inside each of us to glorify His Son, Jesus Christ.

Matthew 25 tells the story, beginning in verse 14. Three servants were each given different quantities of talents. It was not the amount (or type) of talent which mattered—it was what the servant did with what he had been given. Those who used and grew theirs pleased the master, but the man who buried his displeased the commander.

What are you doing with what has been bestowed upon you? If you do not know your talent, and are wondering what it is, ask God to show you. With prayer, it will be revealed to you. No one is an accident; God did not look down when you were born and exclaim "What am I going to do with this one?" Quite the contrary, He has a distinctive place planned for you, where you will be used for His purpose.

Another misconception I hear is, "What possible difference can one person make?" Millions of people are required to remove their shoes every day. This is the result of one wicked man attempting to destroy an airplane with a bomb hidden in his shoes. His plans were for evil, but God uses the same type of determination for good, possibly through you.

Humans are blessed with many different methods to sense our surroundings. We see with our eyes, hear with our ears, smell with our noses, touch with our skin, and taste with our tongues. However, the eyes feed us more information, continually, than any of the others. As a result, we tend to give more recognition and power to what we see over what is hidden.

The head (face, mouth, eyes, ears, and nose) is the most seen portion of the body, but is it the most important? The heart muscle is hidden from everyone (other than perhaps a thoracic surgeon) deep inside the chest, but is it useless? In some places it is indecent to show the bicep of the left arm; does that make it more or less important than the right? What about the big toe, usually hidden deep inside shoes? These are each intricate parts the whole body requires to perform and function to its full capacity.

We are inclined to believe people we see evangelizing, people who have large, well-publicized ministries, are of much greater importance to the Kingdom than those of us who witness to just a few. No! We are all part of the body of Christ. It takes many different parts, shapes, sizes, and colors to make up each body. God values each soul and loves each child He has created.

The face may be seen most, but more important than a big toe? If you do not have a big toe, you will have great difficulty in standing or walking because it creates balance for the rest of the body. Without it, you will repeatedly fall down and scrape your face. No one ever brags about what a beautiful big toe they have, but it is a very important part of the body. You may quietly share and reflect God's love, but never doubt you are an intricate, vital part to the Kingdom of God.

Let's look at examples of where God's word shows us where He used some of the unlikeliest, imperfect people to accomplish His plans. As we read in the Bible, we find God does not utilize those who have it all together. He draws on flawed individuals whose hearts are willing to be used. It is the state of the heart with which He is most concerned. Even with limitations and defects, much can be accomplished with an eager attitude and God. If He waited until His subjects obtained perfection, He could never use any of us. Maybe David, Peter, Moses, or Paul, men held up for examples of godly grandeur, were exceptions....

King David: an adulterer, a liar, a murderer

In Acts 13:22, God calls David "*a man after my own heart.*" However, my Bible also tells me he was not perfect. It begins in 2 Samuel 11: One night King David saw Bathsheba taking a bath. He called her to the palace and initiated an adulterous affair. A few weeks later, Bathsheba contacted him; she had conceived a child. David went to elaborate measures to hide what he had done, and eventually had her husband killed. His actions confirm him as an adulterer, a liar, and a murderer. David repented and God used him in very powerful ways.

Peter: guilty of assault, a coward

Look at Peter who was considered Jesus' right-hand man, but his character is one to which we find we can easily relate. Peter was able to accomplish something no other man has ever done. He walked on water (Matthew 14:29) to reach Jesus! However, the instant he dropped his eyes from the Savior's, he lost faith and sank. Peter again found his faith and *knew* who Jesus was a few chapters later. When asked by Jesus who Peter thought He was, Peter answered, "*You are the Christ, the Son of the living God*" (Matthew 16:15).

"*And I tell you that you are Peter, and on this rock I will build my church, and the gates of Hades will not overcome it*" (Matthew 16:18). When Peter was near Jesus and had been listening to His teachings, Peter held firm in his faith. Jesus knew Peter would be among the faithful disciples who would carry His message to the world. However, Peter also had times when his human side created problems for him. Traditionally, it is accepted that this was the same impetuous Peter who cut the ear of the soldier off at Gethsemane in Matthew 26:51.

Peter was one of the privileged few who accompanied Jesus while praying. But he was baffled and defiant as Jesus told him, "*This very night, before the rooster crows, you will disown me three times*" (Matthew 26:34). Adamantly, Peter argued how he could never reject knowing Christ; he loved Jesus too much. Upon hearing the sound of the cocks' crow, Peter realized Jesus' prediction came true. Although he had been warned, fear of the Roman citizens and what they might do made Peter deny Christ.

The guilt was more than Peter could handle. He did what most of us do when we know we've wronged God—turned and ran. Filled with unbearable guilt, besieged by our actions and hauling unspeakable regret, perhaps he, too, considered suicide.

Then Resurrection Morning arrived. Mary traveled early to the tomb to anoint her Savior's body. An angel of the Lord appeared to her and commissioned her to, "*Go, tell His disciples and Peter, 'He is going ahead of you into Galilee. There you will see Him just as He told you'*" (Mark 16:7, emphasis added). Tell Peter? Why specifically name Peter? Because Christ understood the utter remorse Peter was carrying. He knew even though Peter had been one of His closest friends, Peter would never have come now—unless Christ specifically asked for him. Peter was too buried in the pit of desolation.

I suppose I was very much like Peter. I, too, ran away from the only possible answer to alleviate my sorrow...Jesus. When I heard this verse explained this way, I could hear Jesus say, "and go tell Kay too." And today He is saying, "Go tell_____ (fill in your name). Tell her (or him) I will meet with them too. I have gone before just as I said."

Are you aware of the eleven remaining disciples, the only one who stayed to the final moments at the cross was John? All the others ran away or hid in order to avoid the consequences of being associated with Jesus. Why is it John could stay? He recognized his value in Christ and continually testified to how much he knew Christ loved him. Peter and the rest of Christ's followers were incessantly telling Jesus how much they loved Him. Did you catch the subtle difference between the two sentences? John recognized and accepted Christ's unconditional, unqualified, heavenly love. The other disciples loved Christ with a flawed, human, conditional love. There is a gigantic difference between the two. We can face the future whatever it holds—even death—when we KNOW ourselves to be loved by God.

Moses: a murderer, a liar, a stutterer

Moses was raised in the very palace of the King as a child of privilege and wealth. But on one particular day, he became upset and lost his temper, killing a guard in the King's army. To cover his crime, he hid the body out in the desert. He was also known for having a speech impediment. How could this stuttering murderer ever be of service to God? Our Bible tells us even with his past sins and a disability, Moses stood toe-to-toe with Pharaoh (beginning in Exodus 5) demanding, *"Let God's people go!"* God gave Moses visions of the afflictions which would plague Egypt time and again because the King hardened his heart. Moses, the hotheaded man, led millions of Israelites out of bondage and into the Promised Land. It was also Moses, to whom God himself spoke on multiple occasions, and who received the tablets on which God wrote the Ten Commandments.

Saul: a prolific murderer

Saul: mean, hard hearted, bitter, murderer! We know the early church members were persecuted. They had their houses destroyed; they were put in jail. They were burned at the stake and thrown into arenas with hungry, starved lions. We have no way of knowing exactly how many Christians Saul killed or had put to death, but we do know he had dedicated his life to wiping out the latest fad—Christianity—in his home country. Then one day a light shone so intensely on him, he became blind for several days. God met him right there in the middle of the road on the way to Damascus. Saul's story ends with not only a name, but a spiritual change. Where Saul's purpose in life was to stamp out Christianity, Paul's determination was to take it to everyone possible. Saul became a *"new creature"* named, Paul (Acts 9:4). It was Paul who wrote the scripture given to my ministry. His life was worth nothing to himself except for the purpose of testifying to the grace of Jesus Christ. Paul authored fourteen books of the New Testament and served as a missionary to dozens of countries.

The Bible is peppered with instances of disobedience and sin within God's human instruments:

- **Abraham**, called the "father of many nations" (Genesis 17:4), pressured his wife into swearing she was his sister rather than his wife (Genesis 12:11-13). God still promised him his descendants would be as countless as the stars (Genesis 15:5).

- **Jonah** ran from God (Jonah 1:3) because he did not want to go where he was asked (sound familiar?) but was still the messenger God employed. As a result of Jonah's eventual servitude, the citizens in the city of Nineveh were spared destruction. (Jonah 3:10).
- **Zacchaeus** was a corrupt tax collector (similar to our current IRS) and despised by the average citizen. Nevertheless, Jesus singled him out and asked to visit his house (Luke 19:5) which led to Zacchaeus being a role model of how to repent wicked ways.
- Have you ever been called a *Doubting Thomas*? **Thomas** was one of Jesus' disciples. However, after the resurrection, he would not rely on faith that Christ was alive unless he saw for himself. He had to put his finger in the holes—the wounds Jesus received on the cross, before he would believe Jesus had been raised from the dead (John 20:24-29).
- When Joshua sent two spies into Jericho in preparation for war, **Rahab**, a prostitute, hid them in her tiny apartment (Joshua 2). She is one of only three women named in the lineage of Jesus Christ himself (Matthew 1:5), but if she had not been willing to help God, her family would have perished with the rest of the city.
- **Martha**, Mary's sister, who opened her home to Jesus and His followers, was a worrier (Luke 10:41).
- I smile when I realize He could even use the miracle of raising a dead man, **Lazarus** (John 11), to establish His identity as the Christ.

Many of us have read these stories since childhood, yet we never seem to comprehend the sins they committed. We hold them up as perfect people of God without attaching their disobedient acts. As you read your Bible, this list will expand.

During His ministry, Jesus used what we would consider the *lesser* in society. He looked into their hearts—not at their titles, appearances, or reputations. Certainly God used them. But we look at our transgressions and blindly conclude, "He can't use me!" I suggest if you are not being used, examine your willingness and obedience—not your abilities, social status, or finances. Are you agreeable to being used for the Kingdom?

If you become His instrument, you will be blessed beyond measure. You will discover a life which is fuller and more exciting than anything of which you could ever dream. Somehow we have this idea to be a Christian is restrictive and dull. No! No! No! It is anything but!! In good times and bad, it is never dull!

Be warned, however, there are times when your faith and calling will have detrimental costs, whether in society, family, or even in today's churches. Some may tell you if you are a Christian, your life should be easy. Show me where you find that in the Bible. Instead, Jesus says, *"I have told you these things, so that in me you may have peace. In this world you will have trouble. But take heart! I have overcome the world"* (John 16:33). There are situations almost daily which will challenge your faith. Some appear unassailable; others more like a bump. Jesus said, *"If the world hates you, keep in mind that it hated me first"* (John 15:18).

You may encounter ridicule, anger, bitterness. I personally have been spit upon, had rocks thrown at me, been cursed at, challenged to prove my beliefs, been made fun of, and threatened. People have tried to use intimidation, mocking, and shoving. I have been called a bigot and narrow-minded. I know I am safe in the arms of God; no one can do anything to me without His permission. Unfortunately, when discussing a controversial issue, people react unpredictably.

The way of our world is becoming increasingly hostile towards Christians; they would prefer to obey the easy parts of God's way and ignore the hard portions, calling them "misinterpreted." God's Word stands alone. It is either all true, or all a lie! Jesus was not just a good man or a great prophet. He is either who He says He is (the Son of God, the Messiah) or He is a liar. It is one or the other. Be prepared with your answer, you may be asked to make a choice one day.

Either way, God is still God—and He is the author and finisher of our faith. *"You, dear children, are from God and have overcome them, because the one who is in you is greater than the one who is in the world"* (1 John 4:4). Be strong, stand on your convictions and trust. Find comfort in this: God does not call the equipped; He equips those He calls. Do not rely on yourself but on Him. He will give you all you need at exactly the moment you need it. Often, it feels like the twelfth chime of the midnight clock, but He is never late for His purposes.

꧁꧂

What happened to the hardened person who was so proud of the fact she had never cried in five years? Where is the woman who was so self-serving, the one with no value and no opinions of worth? The portion of my life which once played as a movie filled with hopelessness and depression has been placed on a back shelf in my mind. Many frames of it, the adultery, abortion, the life of self-absorption...these are only a part of me. They do not define who I am! By God's grace, an old rugged cross, Jesus' sacrifice and resurrection, I am now filled with a message of hope, love, and forgiveness.

Scores of women and men wait, praying to hear their secret sin is pardonable too. Incalculable numbers of people eagerly hope against hope someone will be willing to help—and not be repulsed. They sit behind closed doors, in the pews, in front of students, leading Bible studies, anticipating someone who completely understands and offers them steps of healing instead of remarks of scorn and guilt, they think they so richly deserve. Will you step forward and be ready when God moves and uses you?

꧁꧂

The journey He promised me in Washington D.C., one unforgettable night, is still in progress. I pack and repack my suitcase with the physical needs, but also with those experiences He has assigned me to share. Since my first trip for Remembering S.A.R.A. Ministries International, God has opened up countless doors and incredible opportunities for me to give my testimony domestically (such as speaking at a forum at the White House) and internationally (at a forum for the United Nations). I take no acclaim for any of it; none of these offers or doors could ever be opened by human hands unaided. The finances are beyond what Doug and I can manage alone.

The entire ministry is directed by a Heavenly Father who has commissioned me; to personally take any of the credit for what has been accomplished would be shear foolishness. To God be all the glory for all He has done:

- A woman in Australia walks up and admits for the first time ever of her abortion. With a death-like grip, she asks for help. The look in her eyes says, "Please, no one else has offered hope. Don't turn me away!"
- The beautiful young girl in South America sobbing, says, "Today I am a new creature. Wear this black beaded ring when you share. Always remember: you made a difference in me." Considering the poverty she was in, it may have been the only ring she owned.
- The bear hug from the man in The Philippines who wants to find his girlfriend who kept their baby when he walked away. He wants to be a responsible father to his abandoned daughter.
- The victim of a rape over 20 years ago, still struggling with her identity, finds healing and forgiveness, transforming from a caterpillar into a butterfly, physically and spiritually, at the discovery of who she truly is in Christ.
- The grandparents struggling to forgive and help their daughter forgive herself, for the grandchild they will never see this side of heaven.
- The woman conceived in rape, stands proudly and says, "How I was conceived is not the essence of who I am. I am a human being, and I have value and purpose too."
- The young 15 year-old girl, after seeing an ultrasound, her eyes drowning in their own tears, quietly says, "I was going to kill it, but I will give him life instead. Then, even harder, I will give him to a family who can love and give him all I can't."

The list is inexhaustible, and may never be fully known in this world. The freedom found in Christ is transforming. God's Word is alive and working when we share it:

So it is My Word that goes out from My mouth:
It will not return to me void, but will
accomplish what I desire and achieve the
purpose for which I sent it.
                                        Isaiah 55:11

Not always are we blessed to see the results of the seeds we sow, but when we get a peak of the conversions, words will never sufficiently describe it. I have been blessed above and beyond anything I could have imagined since I whispered "Use me, Lord. Just use me!" Traveling the world and sharing my secrets and His grace, helping others to demolish the walls which held them captive, the experiences are more spine-tingling than anything I have ever encountered, ever.

❦

I shuddered at revealing my story to the whole world in a book. How do you accurately articulate something so important and unique to others, something they may never have experienced? How can you make them fully understand? Written words on bleak, white pages without intonation are inadequate to share the peace, love, and forgiveness I have found. I am not capable of portraying accurately the picture which gives others hope to change their lives. It is imperative each of you understand there is forgiveness for **anyone**; I am nothing special outside of Him. Hearing or reading my immorally wrong life will never impact or change anything without the influence of the Holy Spirit. God has brought me through my trials so I would be a stepping stone for others to find freedom in Him as well.

It would be after many tears, times of fasting, and lying prostrate on the floor asking for a way, God would gently reveal

His answer. In His quiet loving way I heard, "Kay, you think too highly of yourself, it will not be your words, but My Holy Spirit, which will convict them to see the truth. Just write down what I have placed on your heart." I have tried, to the best of my humble ability, immersed in prayer along the way, to do God's bidding. My hope and dream is to turn every person who reads it to the light of the SONshine.

The puzzle is yet to be completed as the pieces continue to fall into place. Remembering S.A.R.A. Ministries International is small in comparison to many ministries but continues to grow. Whether it reaches one, one hundred, or thousands, each one has value in the Kingdom. God has created opportunities for me to speak on TV and radio, in legislatures and Parliaments, at The White House, in United Nation Forums, appear in newspapers, colleges, and even prisons—so many incredible places. Remembering where and how it all began and how I limited the scope of my ministry with my short vision, I leave it up to the One to whom this ministry belongs in which direction we go next. I am trying to learn not to outguess God's plan.

While I traveled for weeks at a time, not once did Doug complain. Once, he was asked if he ever wanted to just tell me "No! Stay home." Laughingly, he responded, "I've seen the need, and I know what she does. She's called. If you think I am going to argue with God, forget it!" It is my prayer one day Doug can travel with me and share the joy this ministry brings so many.

Chapter Twenty

"Kay, you have cancer." Though I tried, I could not catch my breath; the oxygen had been whisked from the room. My head was suddenly swarmed with fog. My mind spun as I tried to comprehend the words the doctor just uttered. The unexpected diagnosis of a very aggressive ovarian cancer (Stage 3a uterine papillary serous carcinoma) was sudden and unexpected. Remembering S.A.R.A. Ministries International has been moving like a freight train taking life-saving medicine to an epidemic outbreak. All of a sudden, around a blind corner, a rockslide covered the tracks and halted all momentum. Promises not kept, friendships not settled, and future plans were all now in limbo. My knees, which were strong seconds ago, swiftly buckled in fear. I am sure the blood drained from my face, and I was visibly shaken.

Then tranquility took over. A peace I cannot describe entered, one which should pass understanding and explanation, except Philippians 4:7 tells me it comes from Jesus. It took a little time for me to absorb the impact of the doctor's statement, but I knew I was safe in the arms of my Lord. "Well, let's do whatever is needed. I have things to do and Remembering S.A.R.A. Ministries International trips planned."

Cancer is such a part of life in the United States these days. According to cancer.org, one of every three women and one in every two men will develop some kind of cancer in his or her lifetime. Everyone knows someone who has either had it, or is currently suffering with it. But when the doctor tells you, *you* have cancer, the impact of those few words is indescribable. It is not a friend, a co-worker, or someone who is part of the Wednesday night bingo set. This time, I could not say, "I'll be praying for you," walk away, and go home to normality. Oh, no! Not this time. It was me...Me!

Suddenly I was plunged in a continuous battle, twenty-four hours a day, seven days a week, with a disease which does not care about family, dreams, skin color, age, or social status. Recognizing about half the instances of cancer are fatal, life became precious and was quickly put in perspective.

Denial was the first step, but all-too-soon, reality hit like an atomic bomb blast. The doctors warned me, "You may feel out of control as you go through your treatment; so take control of whatever you can." Within a very short ten days, I found myself in an operating preparation room awaiting surgery to remove anything which might possibly contain the deadly and dreaded disease.

After surgery, I looked at my home and all the treasured things in it. For all the importance previously placed on these items, they were now worth nothing; they were just things. My family and friends always talk about what will happen tomorrow. Without a blink, but, all of a sudden, even just a few minutes shared with these loved ones were precious. At one time my life was too busy to spend time in the Word and prayer. I promised myself I would do it tomorrow; these times alone with the Lord were now to be an unwavering part of my life, each and every day. My priorities were changed; my sights set on much more eternal concerns. The cancer altered my values in an instant.

My best friend had just died of cancer a few months before my diagnosis, after a fierce seven year scuffle, and I was intensely aware of what might lay ahead of me. She may have lost her battle with the disease, but she, without question, won the war of faith! She stayed faithful in dark times as well as the victorious times. She remained strong with the Lord whether her pronouncement was of the reoccurring plague, or the thrill of hearing the words: "It is in remission." The light of Jesus shone brightly in her life, without hesitation, and she continually witnessed to others throughout her ordeal.

Someone once told me, "Witness with all which is within you, and if all else fails, talk to them about Jesus." She did both and I can unequivocally state she is reaping her rewards as I write. I wanted to use her as a role-model for the hard times in front of me.

⚜

My personality requires structure, so I examined all the options and took control of any possibilities in which I might be able to influence the outcome. I began making a record of the dos and don'ts by which I would try to live. I set a direction by making a plan.

Here is my list:
1.   Christ is the big "C." I would never capitalize the word cancer ever again.
2.   I would not ask "Why me?" but instead chose, "Why not me?" God owes me nothing. He already gave me His Son, voluntarily. What more could I expect from Him? I reasoned if I questioned this basic truth, why had I never questioned why He put me in America? He could have easily deposited me in Africa, to struggle daily for meager food and inadequate shelter. Yet, in the worst of times should I not succeed? I was confident He would understand. I assure you in extreme times of pain or nausea, I did fail. But He was faithful.
3.   I made a conscious decision I would never refer to having a "bad" day. On those days when I lay on the bathroom floor, too sick to pull myself back to bed, due to the chemo treatments, I would call it a "faith" day, because it would only be with faith I could get through it. I determined this was an instance where I was to practice "*giving thanks in all circumstances*" (1 Thessalonians 5:18). I could be thankful I was still alive and able to praise God in both the good and the bad times.
4.   No matter what, this would be a win-win situation. I would win either by beating this uncaring, relentless disease or I would go home to be with my Lord. However, if I was to leave this world, I would go out witnessing with all that was within

me...all the way...demonstrating that which I had vocally claimed publicly. Either way, I would WIN! I claimed over and over to myself, my friends, and my loving family, "*By His wounds we are healed*" (Isaiah 53:5).

Unfortunately, I failed, dismally, time after time, to live up to my extremely aggressive expectations. Yet, I can guarantee I tried my humanly best to live up to the hopes I set for myself. I have no doubts my loving Savior understood my efforts because He could see my heart, especially those days I tried and was unsuccessful.

I waged war with everything in me to remain in charge of my destiny. Soon I found myself thrust into feeling helpless as I sat there for hours on end while the methodical drip of the chemotherapy was administered in my arm. The medical staff who helped were simply angels in disguise as nurses. They made me feel special, like some important executive, never behaving as if I were just the newest member of a sad statistic or a file number. They always made every effort to make me comfortable, by being supportive and treating me as if I was the only one in the room who mattered.

Just a few days after the first treatment, I discovered an area in which I would have absolutely no control. Clumps of my hair began to fall out. I walked into the living room where Doug was reading the newspaper and announced, "I'm getting dressed and going to Super Cuts. I will not stand idly by and watch my hair fall out! I will take it into my own hands and not allow these merciless treatments to decide the timing." Moments later, tears rolled down my face as I watched the reflection of the shy beautician shaving my head. I slipped on the wig I had purchased earlier to cover my baldness before heading home. Even Doug would not see me stripped of my crown of hair for a couple weeks.

Even in the midst of all the trials and tribulations, humiliation and humbleness, I found times of humor. Brent, my grandson, plays baseball and I wanted to support him. Typical of league games, there were multiple fields being used, and I could not locate the correct field. So I called Madeline on my cell phone to come get me. Soon I saw her and my adorable five-year-old granddaughter coming towards me. Krysten was running ahead of her mother, and as she drew near, waving frantically, she yelled loudly, "Grandma, Grandma, did you bring your hair too?" Everyone within hearing range stopped to gawk, wondering at the strange question. Yet all I could do was laugh. It reminded me that my hair was an accessory, not the essence of my being.

Suzie traveled to visit us for a full family retreat up in the beautiful mountains not far from our home. The first morning there, Suzie took her shower and came out to the family in her housecoat. Looking directly at me she inquired, "Mom, do you have a comb and shampoo I can borrow? I forgot mine back at the house." Everyone burst into laughter as she stood there, not sure whether to laugh at herself or feel guilty for such a non-consequential question.

Unfortunately, the long unforgettable days where I would lie on the cold, hard bathroom floor, too frail and sick to get up out of my own vomit, outnumbered the light-hearted and good days. Doug was there, encouraging me, holding me, helping me in those extremely hard times. Praying together, we were both doggedly determined cancer would not take me from this world.

Months later I would hear the treasured words "Your cancer is gone!" spoken. Outside of assurance of my salvation, they have to be some of the most beautiful words I have ever heard. I wanted to run and shout to the world, rent a huge flashing sign on Broadway to advertise, "I BEAT IT!!"

As I jubilantly walked out of the doctor's office, my happiness was momentarily put on hold. The chemotherapy room was next door, and I looked inside to see several of the patients with whom I had sat and talked. My heart ached as I wondered what words the doctor would be sharing with them. Their battles were as real as mine; in some cases the path to healing had been more invasive. What would be their final diagnoses? And what about their souls?

While in treatment, I knew it would be unacceptable for me to openly share my story. The nurses administer drugs to make you drowsy, to make time go more quickly. So I took my ministry business cards and a few copies of my one-page testimony and laid them on the table next to my chair. If someone was interested, they could pick them up and view them. Several were taken during my treatments. Was it any of these patients who took them? Why? I had hoped someone would approach me to talk, but it did not happen. So I had to turn it over to God to let Him use them as He wanted. There is always an opportunity to share, whether by words, by actions, or by a paper left deliberately behind.

No more will the wicked invade you; they will be completely destroyed.
                                    Nahum 1:15

When I was in combat fighting for my life, I recited this verse, which God revealed to me, often. When I am asked if I fear the return of cancer, I will always end my statement with: "Adversity will not visit me a second time." I am over two years clean, and I will not audibly or inaudibly claim any return of it in my body.

Chapter Twenty-One

I am involved in a new combat as I write, one to save my vision. About five years ago I was told I have wet macular degeneration (notice I did not capitalize its name either). This condition is when the blood vessels in the back of your eye become aggressive for unknown reasons and breaks down the back wall of the eyeball. Blood leaks into your eye causing a large dark spot in the middle of the visual images, eventually causing blindness. I have lost seventy percent of my vision in my right eye (making me legally blind in that eye). There are no accepted remedies for this degenerative disease. However, the doctors are experimenting with a medication normally used for prostate cancer in men. I receive injections directly into the pupil of my eyes. Thanks to God—The Divine Physician—and a wonderful Ophthalmologist, my right eye is stable at this time. However, about three months ago my good (left) eye has also begun to weaken. I am currently battling for clear sight in it.

We scurry through our days concerned about life and completely miss the Creator's handiwork. Knowing my sight is in peril, I spend more time lingering on beautiful scenes, committing them to memory. We take an annual evening drive through our town, enjoying the Christmas light displays. We go with Kevin and his family, and take a huge thermos of hot chocolate and several bags of sliced apples. This year, it is incredible how much more intently I notice the brilliant colors. Sunsets of incredible beauty, I try to paint into my memory. I often take a second, long look at the faces of loved ones and at the majesty of the world around. I believe in my healing, but the idea of the possibility of no sight makes me far more aware of everything around me. Yet I will trust Him.

＊＊＊＊＊

In 2005, a prophecy was given to me: I would be diagnosed and doctors would tell me they could do no more for me, but God would intervene. I remember after the meeting hurrying home to Doug. He was lounging in his chair casually reading his newspaper. I pushed it aside and crawled up into his lap, sharing what had occurred. I clearly remember stating, "I think I can take anything except losing my sight. I do not think I could handle that."

Now looking back, I have often wondered since, if like Job, God has given Satan permission to try me. By my own acknowledgement, he is doing to me what I most fear. I remember what the Word says about the power of the tongue, *"The tongue has the power of life and death and those who love it will eat its fruit"* (Proverbs 18:21). Am I eating the fruit of what I suggested?

In all honesty, I awake with panic attacks in the middle of the night. Startled because the air around me becomes so extremely tight, I can scarcely breathe. I clamber to find the light switch to see into the darkness and become aware of my surroundings. It is hard to describe the absolute feelings of defenselessness and terror I experience. Once the light is on, and I realize it is not the permanent darkness I fear, I usually proceed to a large room or go outside to relieve the claustrophobia.

Then the little voice inside from the enemy asks me, "What will you do when the light switch will not bring back the light and relieve the fear? Then what? It is inevitable you will experience total darkness, permanently, soon, you know." I feel so vulnerable and powerless when this happens. The enemy is attempting, unsuccessfully, to use my fear to rip me apart from my faith.

I will sing a song to God. I recite scripture to restore my calmness. *"What I tell you in the dark, speak in the daylight; what is whispered in your ear, proclaim from the roofs. Do not be afraid of those who kill the body but cannot kill the soul.*

Rather, be afraid of the one who can destroy both body and soul in Hell" (Matthew 10:27-28). I will do anything so the enemy cannot stay around. In the presence of Jesus' name, he must flee. I need to come to a place at peace with whatever lies ahead. I am getting there, slowly. God gave me the courage to face my children with my long hidden secret. God has given me the courage to speak to millions of people about abortion. God can give me the courage to be at peace with this situation. I pray I can be all He wants, whatever the outcome. I do not know what tomorrow may bring, but I trust the one who holds it in His hands.

Right now I stand on the promise He will give me all I need and never more than I can carry. In the episode with cancer, I would be able to win, no matter what happened. However, the idea of complete dependency on others due to the unyielding darkness, blindness, is unbalanced. If the disease wins my eyesight, there is no reward for me. Daily, sometimes minute by minute, I battle with fear. There are 365 "fear not's" in the Bible, one for every day of the year. I need every single one and speak them out loud claiming peace and victory.

When I measure the few years on this earth in darkness against the billions and billions and billions of years in the glory of heaven, I am willing to submit to His hands. His mercies are new every morning and I am His...whatever happens. Not as easily done as said, but I press forward to what lies ahead. In my very present need I know He is able and will never forsake me. I am His bond servant and He is my master. Although I may feel lonely, I will NEVER be alone.

⚬⚭⚮⚯⚬⚭⚮⚯⚬

As before, I try never to end talking about this new challenge without something which will show my faith in the God I serve. I promised He could use me as He sees fit; I am His. The words came easy that night years ago. However, adversity has now stepped in and I'm facing the very possibility of my most horrible fear becoming reality. Where is my faith? Right here! Inside me! It is not about having sufficient faith, or I would be healed.

Paul had enough faith to perform miracles. He also had a thorn of some type in his flesh, but God could use him to a greater degree by leaving it there. I believe with all my heart God understands my fear, and He also sees my heart's desire to serve Him in every aspect of my life. He understands my human frailty and weaknesses. Should He choose to entrust me with lost sight, I know He died so I might live, and live abundantly (John 10:10, KJV). I will be healed, whether in this life or the next. So I will surrender to whatever the outcome my Lord feels He can use the best for His kingdom...miracle, stability, or loss. I WILL TRUST HIM.

God wants us to be confident in the knowledge He desires the best for His children. While we humans only see the short term and local events, God assures us He knows how all the events weave together for His good and His purposes. *"For I know the plans I have for you," declares the Lord, "plans to prosper you and not to harm you, plans to give you hope and a future"* (Jeremiah 29:11). I believe there is much to be seen which human eyes cannot show you. So I wait for His plan with expectancy every day.

Doug assures me as he pulls me close, my ministry is not reliant on my eyes but on my testimony. If needed, Doug will accompany me on my Remembering S.A.R.A. Ministries International trips. When I am ready to get on stage and share, he will lead me up the stairs and over to the microphone, then be waiting to lead me off stage again. Whatever the future holds, we will continue the ministry until God says it is done. Despite my failed, miserable history, God has given me an extraordinary man as a helpmate. He seems to be able to lift me up at just the right time. Doug has this uncanny gift to know just when to talk, and when to leave it alone. It is easy to follow and lean on him when I know where his guidance comes from: God. Doug is my stalwart Christian Marine husband, without whom I would be lost.

I kept my condition secret from most people for several years, probably because of pride. God made it clear just recently, should He choose to do a miracle, who would believe? Since I have kept the condition from public knowledge, no one could witness it. Someone watching me, even now, will need to see the faith I profess in action. So I have shared with church, family, friends, and in my witnessing. Not an easy task but I know God has a purpose for requiring it of me.

The future lies ahead, uncertain as always. We make plans like we are promised tomorrow, but there is no guarantee we will see it. Until the end of time, it will be filled with challenges. The most crucial part is not our circumstances but how we deal with them. We need to try and view them from God's perspective not our own. "Remember," as my pastor always says, "problems on this earth are 'itty-bitty' compared to the GREAT BIG GOD WE SERVE."

Honestly, though, I struggle...really struggle. Permanent darkness, losing my independence, it is more terrifying at times than I can express. Yet, I will praise Him. Even when I was diagnosed with cancer, I never believed that was the ailment of which the prophecy spoke. Instead, I am convinced it concerns my sight. In which case, I will be healed in God's perfect way and plan. I have been given a scripture for this troubled time and it can be found in Psalms 27:13:

> *I am still confident of this: I will see the*
> *goodness of the LORD in the land of the living.*

As with important scriptures given to me before, it is plastered all throughout my house, car and in areas I find myself daily...crazy places like my steering wheel, the front of the coffee pot, my checkbook, and on my shower wall. I interpret this scripture this way: I am CONFIDENT I will **SEE** the goodness of the LORD in the land of the living. I know my sight will not be taken from me while I still live.

I try to calmly accept this verse as I interpret it, but to try to out-guess God would be efforts foolishly wasted. I did that once before. While I was married to Gary, I was given a verse: "*Do not fear, for I am with you; Do not anxiously look about you, for I am your God. I will strengthen you; surely, I will help you. I will uphold you with My right hand*" (Isaiah 41:10, NAS). I had tried to guess what God meant at that time. I thought He was going to restore my marriage if I stopped anxiously watching Gary's affair with Ellen. Instead, He helped me through the situation and gave me an inner strength. He pulled me back to Him and holds *every* aspect of my life in His hands now. So, I attempt not to be anxious about the outcome and rest calmly in His arms.

Recently, a pastor friend from another church denomination offered to come and anoint both of my eyes. Suzie flew in; all my children and their families gathered in our living room for the simple and encouraging service. After reading promises from the Word, he prayed and placed Cedars of Lebanon oil, brought from the Holy Land, on my closed eye-lids. He dedicated my eyes to the God who gave me life and to whom I gave my life. Healing may be in this world, but without doubt, will be in the next. I am to continue declaring my scriptures and believe God wants the best for me; healing is always an option.

Claiming this victory over my current battles requires a personal relationship with my Savior, not a specific religion. I am persuaded Satan is not bothered with "religious" people. The Pharisees were religious, ritually going through the motions of worship, more concerned about legalistic issues than with a deep-rooted understanding of what it means to know Jesus personally. I believe the enemy is delighted with this type of Christian. The relationships Satan worries about are the ones who have an intimate, cherished bond with our Lord—the kind where you talk to Him about everything, listen for His answers, praise Him in all things, at all times...even when you do not like nor understand the outcome.

The enemy pays attention when you do something God has required of you, and, even if you do not want to carry out your orders, out of love, you obey. When you have a Kingdom mentality of desiring to do His will, even over your own, without any payment, and have the deep understanding of the difference between knowing Him and *KNOWING HIM*, that is what the enemy fears. As sinners, we need that kind of relationship with Jesus. Walking with Him is an ongoing journey which is renewed every single day.

I rest assured, my Heavenly Father loves me! Even at my worst, He loved me. My salvation does not depend on things I do. I am saved **for** good works **not by** them (Ephesians 2:8-9). If salvation could be earned by good works, then God sending His Son as a sacrifice to die for our sins was pointless. Nothing God does is pointless, and everything He does is filled with His undeniable love for us. God sent His Son into our world to save us from our own destruction. I do not have any illusions about God being a jealous and just God who requires certain things from us. He will hold me accountable for my actions, but I also continually remind myself: It is not how we start this life, but how it ends which is most important.

Remember Moses (murderer), David (adulterer), Rahab (prostitute), Peter (coward)...me (murderer and adulteress). Before God began to use our lives, inadequate vessels that we are, we were condemned to an eternity in Hell. But He desires to spend eternity with as many of us as possible, including you. If you do not have a personal relationship with Jesus Christ, start one today. You are not beyond redemption. If you are reading this book, then you are still breathing—it is not too late. Right now can be a "new beginning" for YOU. He is more than enough! I know because I am His...and He is mine.

For I am confident of this unchanging truth, with all my inadequacies, weaknesses, blemishes, and uncountable sins, of this I am absolutely sure:

In all these things, we are more than conquerors, through HIM who loved us. I am convinced that neither death nor life, neither angels nor demons, neither the present nor the future, nor any powers, neither height nor depth nor anything else [including blindness] in all creation, will be able to separate us [me] from the [unconditional] love that is in Jesus Christ our Lord.

Romans 8:37-39 (Kay's version)

The End

My Story, GOD'S Book

Although I have always enjoyed writing, a personal book would have been on the bottom of my *to do* list. Even years ago, when I was told it would happen, I scoffed at the idea of such a revealing journey. I knew I did not have the financial means to publish a book. Then, when facing the imminent threat of death, I felt compelled to be obedient to what I knew God had been asking of me. Sins I denied (even to those exclusive people who knew them to be true) for decades, have been further cleansed in the process of disclosure. It was an emancipating three-plus year project, more rewarding and fulfilling than I could have dreamed.

God tenderly showed His hand to me in rather curious ways as I began this experience. When word spread about the pending book, Linda, the wife of the pastor who was instrumental in my healing, volunteered to edit it for me. She asked, "Didn't you know, I have a Master's Degree in creative writing?" I had no clue. Ka-ching! Money saved! Thank you, Lord.

I felt I needed to have someone who read a great deal to evaluate it for flow and impact, before I gave it to Linda. DeeDee and I talked about who we knew that read a lot. We both agreed: Carrie Lynn was an avid reader; she would be perfect. Carrie graciously and readily agreed. Several days later, she called and offered her services to help take this from a "good book" to a "great book." She once worked for a publisher and was familiar with some of the process. I had no idea. God, again, had paved the way. Ka-ching, again!

Next, there was a quiet, attractive 16-year-old girl who attended our small church for just a few short weeks. Being bored with some aspects of the service, she etched away randomly on the weekly bulletin. One of the cleaning ladies mentioned what an amazing gift Hannah had. I approached her about doing a cover, offering to pay for her talent. She shyly agreed to do the illustration, but added that no pay would be required—the acknowledgement in the book would be a great help in gaining credibility with a college majoring in arts. After talking with her about the contents of the book and a couple ideas I had, she eagerly began to work. Her God-given forte is evident on the front of this book. May she always bless the Lord with the remarkable gift He has given her. Ka-ching, once again!

I was trying to be obedient in what HE wanted of me, despite my shame of being exposed. HE was honoring my submission by opening doors I had no idea how to find or open.

Carrie Lynn then revealed her job was in the design department. She and her contacts professionally produced the book cover with no out-of-pocket expenses.

While visiting the local pregnancy center, where I once trained in counseling, one of the co-directors asked how the book was going. Then she asked me who was writing the forward. I smiled and explained I did not even know I needed one! I looked her straight in the eye and continued, "Well, I guess you are. God seems to bring me what I need when I need it. Would you do me the honor?" She had never written one, but reluctantly agreed. When she submitted the final product, Linda admitted to me the forward was a far better work than she had ever written. She said the words "just flowed," and she was astonished at the outcome. The Lord was speaking through her. And…Ka-ching, yet again.

My children all read this book before it went to print. I wanted to allow them a voice in how the events were portrayed and a chance to offer suggestions. For some, it was a more difficult request than it was for others, but they all read it and offered thoughts to enhance it, encouraging the completion of the book. I would have been torn if any one of them had balked at the stories exposed. It was God! Only God!

While in process of writing, I found it necessary that a pen and paper should always be within an arm's reach—at any given time. I never knew exactly when, or how, God would give me a part of the book. God gave me the example about the volcano in the shower one Sunday morning when I was already late for church. He woke me in the middle of the night to reveal the description of the Prodigal Son [Daughter], the ring, robe, and shoes. I found myself struggling to explain in words—the ideas conveyed in the closing paragraphs of the book; during prayer, they, too, came at the exact time they were needed.

Several very dear friends have also added their input with their talents. I am extremely humbled they asked to have a part in this ministry without compensation or acknowledgement. May our Lord bless them for hearing HIS voice and offering their talents.

God gave me a list of people to ask to endorse the book. Some of the people are far more important than I. God has gone before in this as well and has paved the way.

It has not been disclosed to me at this time how this book is to be published. After HIS constant guiding of this book, I am fully confident it will be published by someone whom HE has already chosen. Any funds necessary, I am positive HE has already provided, but has not chosen to show me yet. My hands are inadequate compared to HIS greatness. I do not have the resources to place this book into your hands as you hold it today. But God does!

There is one thing of which I am certain: this is **God's book**! It is a story of redemption and forgiveness, as lived by me, but God is, and has always been, in control. HE will orchestrate it in HIS way and HIS time. This is HIS! Praise be to the name of our LORD!

K

Doug
Celebrating A Life Spent In Service

As this book was headed for print, my husband Doug was called home for Christmas. He was an immeasurable part of my life, ministry, and this book, as you have read. We held a "Celebration" of his first Christmas with Jesus with praises, singing, and smiles (and tears) of his effects on lives he touched. It is with a strong faith in our Lord, yet, a shattered heart filled with loss, I honor Doug with this book.

Doug was the example of a humble servant. He was the one who did the mundane things like paying bills, handling the media issues, fixing my frozen computer, proof reading, and watching after all the things at home. No fanfare, no glitz, just serving as he felt God intended. He would encourage me to stretch...step out...go. While I traveled the world, he simply did the little things required to keep things smooth here. While I saw sights and met new friends, he simply prayed for me as he shampooed the rugs and did all the little backup things no one ever notices or thinks of. No big thank you for him, no applause. He always said he had seen God's hand in what I do, and he wouldn't argue with God. And this man of God just stayed in the background and did what to others might consider nothing or insignificant. Not an easy task for a proud twenty-one year Marine.

He promised to be my eyes if mine failed, telling me; "God doesn't need your eyes, I'll get you on stage, he needs your testimony. And now what?? I find myself at a crossroads. At times like these, we either believe and live what we claim, or throw it all away and just quit. And some do just that. Doug would never allow me to quit before when I felt beaten and discouraged. With him gone, I now lean more than ever before on my faith. God is who He is as the Bible states or He is not. I can attest to God being very near to me right now as it feels like the whole world is crumbling around.

Since his departure to heaven, three people have rededicated or committed their lives to Christ that I know of. Doug would be thrilled to have such reactions to his new eternal address. Several others watched as his praises grew and his body grew faint; that too left an indelible mark in witnessing.

The future seems pale and uncertain. But of this I AM MORE THAN CERTAIN. HE who holds tomorrow, also is holding me right now. And with tears and a heart that feels absolutely broken, I choose Jesus. To continue to serve as my Doug did; not always understanding, but with joy and a knowing hope, HE will be my guide. Doing whatever HE calls upon me to do, go where HE wants me to go. S.A.R.A Ministries is not over; it has much to do, just as there is much for you to complete as well. Determine this day whom you will serve. BUT AS FOR ME AND MY HOUSE, WE WILL SERVE THE LORD.

Jesus said to her, *"I am the resurrection and the life. He who believes in me will live, even though he dies, and whoever lives and believes in me will never die."*

Do you believe this?? (John 17:25 & 26)

YES, With all my being!!!! (as answered by K)

Appendices

Some people may need an idea of where to begin writing the letters of forgiveness. I have included my letters here to provide a starting point for you. These are as I wrote them, misspelling and incorrect grammar included. Yours need to come from your heart. You have your own convictions; write what God tells you.

My Letters:
    A. Letter to God
    B. Letter to Sara
    C. Letter to Gary

Letter to God

Feb. 16, 2003

Dear God,

I have been asked to write a letter to you explaining how I feel about you and my relationship with you. After beginning that is not as easy as it sounds.

My first thoughts upon starting was how awesome, patient and loving you are to one like myself. One who disregarded your laws, as I numerously sinned against you as I "did it my way." Yes, the word is true. You are slow to anger, quick to forgive, Thank Goodness!

More times than I can count I have thrown your word back in your face, yet as many times forgiven and redeemed me to yourself. You have taken the broken and darkness of my turning and made me whole and new again and again.

I have repented and I know by your word I am forgiven. It is so simple to do and yet so extremely hard. To turn away and then ask for forgiveness, when Satan reminds me, "Who do you think you are?" You are not good enough! Look at all you've done against him!" I remind myself he is the father of lies. There are times things go wrong in my life & it seems as though you have left me & my prayers only bounce back into my face from the ceiling above. I know the Bible says not to go on feelings but on faith. Doubts flood in and I search myself to see what am I being punished for this time. Again, I know to keep my eyes on you and not on the problem. To remember that all things work for good according to his purpose. That nothing! NOTHING!! can separate me from your love. It is not what life hands me but what I do with it that counts in the end. Thank you for the lesson.

Lord, I'm sure I will slip, time & again, though I will strive not to. And you will surely, by your grace, & my repentance give me a new beginning.

My prayer is that you will show

me your will for the rest of my life and I will do a complete all you ask. I need you, Lord, not daily; but minute by minute.... every second. Time is short and the fields are ripe with harvest, I feel you are drawing me out to speak for those with no voice. To share the healing you've offered me. But should you have other plans, make your will clear. Open doors of to place me where I can best used, the boldness to speak your will and the wisdom to be silent.

I know I'm a work in progress. That there is much left to be done in me until the day you call me home. I Love You! Thank you for your grace to me, and I pray that I can share and show the same to others.

Thank you for my family + friends you have provided and the place you have placed me. I will pray daily for them all and especially for those who like myself have false pride and are "Doing It My Way!" Thank you in advance for those persons + situations you

are already putting in my path.
Use me! Use me!

As I look around daily & see the
world and your prophecies being
fulfilled; I see lines being drawn,
lines between people, countries and
culture. God is often called
"politically incorrect," and sin is
embraced.

I know I am redeemed and that
your return may be imminent.
Whether by death or the rapture, I
will be with you soon. Then we
can walk and talk in person, I
can't imagine the joy. Until then
may I walk with you here, where-
ever the path leads.

Love,
K

Letter to Sara

March 19, 2003

Little Baby Sara,

How does one start? Where do I even begin? Saying "I'm sorry," sounds so flippant, so overused, that it has practically lost its meaning. Sara, I would love to be able to go back and undo what I did to you. Through defiance of Gods word, I knowingly took your life. Without any thought of you as a person. I made the selfish determination to about you, so that my lifestyle & growing business would not be interrupted. Please, Baby forgive me.

Sorry, I haven't written this letter to you sooner, nor given you a and date to know you. It must be hurtful to be ignored by your own family. I do take solis in the fact that somehow you understand. Did Jesus sit down with you a talk about it? Did he assure you how much you are loved? Did he explain the cross to you? After a lot of prayer not from just me

but also from your sister, brother
we have named you Dora Marie.
Everyone has agreed that April 13th
will be yours and we will honor
you on that day. You will also
have a place on our family wall.
You were a gift from God
that I threw away. I robbed you
of so many things to numerous to
mention. You had a right to live, a
right to discover the world around
you. To see the sunshine, a clear
blue sky, splash in a mud puddle
with your little boots on, have a
puppy to name, love and play with.
Shop for your prom dress, then that
night with every hair in place, eyes
gleaming when that special boy
arrives. Enjoy an ice cream cone
that somehow gets all over your face.
(wonder what flavor it would have been?)
To celebrate your birthday with the
family enjoying gifts and a cake.
Chase a butterfly as it lites from
one place to another, or pick flowers.
Then I think of the sand castles you
would have built on the water

colors make into pictures that would have hung on the refrigerator. Christmas trees with their sparkling colored lites. You with your sunday school class being an angel in the pagent. And reciting your two lines of scripture at the Easter program. (Would you have remembered them?) Sure you would! All this and so much more I have taken from you, it is a loss I would give anything to change.

Wonder if you would have had my red hair, freckles or blue eyes.... maybe all of them. Would you have loved sports as much as I, or would you rather do music & ballet? What would be your favorite pizza? Would you enjoy Mexican food like the rest of us? Who would be your favorite singer or group? Cooking was never your sisters strong point, what about you?

Your graduations from grade/high school. What special unique talents did God give you? What would you have done with your life? What plans

did he have for you? The list
of regrets goes on and on

Sara, I know you are safe and
happy in God's loving arms, but
Oh how I wish I could hold
you in mine. I've struggled
with your death for a long time
without knowing it but I am in
full knowledge and awareness of
what I have done. I pray it
helps you to know that I am trying
to do all I can to save others like
yourself. I hope you can look down
& say with pride to your friends there,
"That's my mommy. She's on Jesus' side
now trying to save others like us."
If you can, ask Jesus personally to
help me by opening doors of opportunity.
I'm sure he will listen to you.
There have been enough victims like
you, we need not one more.

I may have the wrong date, I
may have the wrong name, but of
this you can be sure, "You are loved
beyond measure." Putting a name and
face to you after all these years
has been wonderful. You now have

an identity of your own, of course, there were tears, but also joy to finally acknowledge you, as you are one of a kind.

Someday, I will be able to give us big hugs & kisses. We will sit and talk for hours about whatever you wish. Please be by the big open gates when I arrive. I'm sure you won't need to hold a sign. We will know each other. When I spoke to your sister D.D. last night, she too wants you to meet her as well. She's always a baby sister. Kevin is a little more reserved, being a typical boy but he said someday he would enjoy your company too. We all love you Baby Dora.

This is not goodbye, it is see you later. I will hold you tightly in my heart until I hold you in my arms personally. Strongly enough I can find it hard to say "Good-bye" now that I have been able to talk to you.

I'll bet you make wherever you are a brighter place. You are my "Special Angel" Dora, & I believe you

make heaven a better and more
beautiful place. You are my cheer-
leader and I know you are watching me.

Until I met you at the gates of
heaven, when I can finally hold
you. I will continue to fight to
save others like yourself.

May God grant me years to help
undo what this nation calls safe,
quick & easy; "abortion."

All my love,
Mommy

Letter to Gary

Sept 14, 2004

Dear Gary,

I am sending you this letter & I pray you will receive it as it is meant. I want to apologize to you for aborting our daughter. I have just come thru a healing Bible Study & plan to speak out publicly against the very thing I did.

One of the requirements of the study was to pray, then give a sex and name to your baby. I have named our baby Sara Maxie & given her the day of April 13th as "her day."

My kids have been told about my abortion & have forgiven me, I pray you will do the same.

The pregnancy center I volunteer at has a wall of recognition & Sara has her own plaque.

I am very sorry for the pain my choice caused you. I pray this letter gives you some type closure & peace as well.

T.

About the Author

Kay Painter is a sinner forgiven—wife, mother, grandmother and great gran—who simply wants to be used by her Savior. She has spoken at forums in the United Nations and the White House, given her testimony on national and international television and radio programs, and has been featured in newspapers and magazine articles. Kay has been on twenty-one international tours in thirteen countries. God is using Remembering S.A.R.A. Ministries International to spread the news of HIS grace.

For contact information, to request a visit, or to obtain additional copies of *From Sin and Sorrow to Service*, please go to www.RememberingSara.org.

Made in the USA
Charleston, SC
10 February 2013